SHABTIS

Illustrated by the Egyptian Collection
in University College, London.

SIR W. M. FLINDERS PETRIE

OXBOW | books
Oxford & Philadelphia

This edition published in the United Kingdom in 2023 by
OXBOW BOOKS
The Old Music Hall, 106–108 Cowley Road, Oxford, OX4 1JE

and in the United States by
OXBOW BOOKS
1950 Lawrence Road, Havertown, PA 19083

Paperback Edition: ISBN 979-8-88857-006-7
Digital Edition: ISBN 979-8-88857-007-4 (epub)

First published by the British School of Archaeology in Egypt, 1935
Facsimile edition published in 1974 by Aris & Phillips Ltd

Oxbow Books is grateful to the Petrie Museum for their collaboration in bringing out these new editions

Printed in the United Kingdom by CMP Digital Print Solutions

For a complete list of Oxbow titles, please contact:

UNITED KINGDOM
Oxbow Books
Telephone (0)1226 734350
Email: oxbow@oxbowbooks.com
www.oxbowbooks.com

UNITED STATES OF AMERICA
Oxbow Books
Telephone (610) 853-9131, Fax (610) 853-9146
Email: queries@casemateacademic.com
www.casemateacademic.com/oxbow

Oxbow Books is part of the Casemate Group

Front cover: Painted wooden shabti of Meh. Provenance unknown, Dynasty 18 (*c.* 1550–1069BC). Petrie Museum UC8824.
Image © Mary Hinkley, UCL Educational Media.

CONTENTS

CHAPTER I

SUBSTITUTE FOR THE BODY

CHAPTER II

THE SUBSTITUTE FOR THE MUMMY

CHAPTER III

THE GROWTH OF THE SHUABTI

CHAPTER IV

GROWTH OF THE SHUABTI FORMULA

CHAPTER V

OTHER TEXTS ON SHUABTIS

CHAPTER VI

FORMS AND MATERIALS OF SHUABTIS

CHAPTER VII

TRANSLITERATIONS

For method of references, see end of Chapter V, p. 10.

LIST OF PLATES

ABBREVIATIONS

Lieb. = LIEBLEIN, Dictionnaire de Noms.
M.C.A. = MASPERO, Cairo.
N.T.N. = NEWBERRY, Theban Necropolis.
N. = PETRIE, Naqada.
P.C.A. = PEET, Cemeteries of Abydos.
P.S.B.A. = Proceedings, Society of Biblical Archaeology.
Rec. = Recueil des Travaux.
R.M.A. = RANDALL MACIVER, El Amrah and Abydos.
U.C. = University College, London.
Z.A.S. = Zeitschrift für ägyptische Sprache.
Museum references, see pl. xv.

PREFACE TO THE 2023 EDITION

In the 1970s, a much-anticipated new series of publications illustrated objects and themes related to the excavations of the archaeologist William Matthew Flinders Petrie (1853–1942) in Egypt, and aspects of the collection of University College London's Petrie Museum of Egyptian and Sudanese Archaeology. A young couple setting up in business in the early 1970s, Aris and Phillips published these works, written by members of the UCL Egyptology Department, in their *Modern Egyptology* series. Building on Petrie's own observations, the authors of these volumes aimed to complete the great task of publishing the Petrie Museum of Egyptian and Sudanese Archaeology's vast collection, and to present some of the research that Petrie himself was not able to address in his own published works during his lifetime. As the current Curator of the Petrie Museum, it is a great privilege for me to support Oxbow Books in their mission to republish the series, which remains a key source of information for all those interested in object-based approaches to the study of the ancient world.

The Petrie Museum, part of University College London (UCL), is home to one of the largest and most significant collections of Egyptian and Sudanese archaeology in the world. Free to visit, this extraordinary collection tells stories about the lives of ordinary people who lived along the Nile Valley thousands of years ago. Originally set up as a teaching collection, the Petrie Museum comprises over 80,000 objects housed together with an internationally important archaeological archive. It is a collection of world firsts and 'oldests': the oldest woven garment; the oldest worked iron objects; the first known depiction of loom weaving; the oldest known written document about women's health; the earliest veterinary treatise; the oldest will on paper. The Museum has Designated Status from Arts Council England, meaning that it is considered to have outstanding resonance and national cultural significance. The collection has a substantial, visible international reputation for research, supporting hundreds of researchers every year, both remotely and in person.

The Petrie Museum is named after Flinders Petrie, who was appointed in 1892 as the first Professor of Egyptian Archaeology and Philology in the UK at UCL. Over three-quarters of the material in the Museum comes from excavations directed or funded by Petrie, or from purchases he made for university teaching. In 1880 at the age of 26, Petrie travelled to Egypt to survey the Great Pyramid. For the next five decades he was at the forefront of the development of archaeology in Egypt and later in Palestine, and his detailed methodological approach continues to shape the discipline today.

Petrie worked at more sites, with greater speed, than any modern archaeologist: seeing his life as a mission of rescue archaeology, Petrie aimed to retrieve as much information as possible from sites that were shrinking dramatically in size as Egypt modernised during the late 19th and early 20th centuries. He published a large part, but not all, of the finds from his excavations in his illustrated typological volumes, arranged according to object types and themes. Today, much of the Petrie Museum's collection is displayed and stored in a way which reflects these publications: for example, several storage cupboards are dedicated to the material illustrated in the 'Objects of Daily Use' volume, and objects in the drawers are arranged according to the order of the published plates. This offers a unique opportunity for researchers to engage with Petrie's typological and methodical approach to archaeology, as well as with the history of museum collections.

The first catalogue to be published in the *Modern Egyptology* series was *Amarna: City of Akhenaten and Nefertiti* in 1972 by Julia Samson, Petrie Museum Honorary Research Assistant. As official publishers to the UCL Egyptology Department the series went on to produce facsimile reprints of eight of Flinders Petrie's most important site reports and many of his object catalogues, originally published through the British School of Archaeology in Egypt. The substantial annual royalties from these reprints were paid into the 'Petrie Fund' at the time, which provided special grants to students in financial need.

In many ways, the new reprints of this classic series can be seen as the latest layer in a vast 'publication stratigraphy' of the thousands of finds from Flinders Petrie's excavations, which now live in museum collections around the world. On reading these volumes, I hope that readers will also be inspired to learn more about the Petrie Museum collection and its fascinating history.

Dr Anna Garnett
Petrie Museum of Egyptian and Sudanese Archaeology,
University College London
January 2023

PUBLISHER'S PREFACE

Oxbow Books is pleased to present this title in our *Classics in Egyptology* series. This series of facsimile re-issues is comprised of two sub-series. The first consists of 16 typological catalogues produced by W.M. Flinders Petrie based on his massive collection of Egyptian artefacts. Mostly excavated by Petrie during many seasons of campaign in the last years of the 19th and early decades of the 20th century, they now reside in the Petrie Museum at University College London. Published between 1898 and 1937 and long out of print, the catalogues were re-issued in facsimile by publishers Aris and Phillips in the 1970s. These were followed in the next 15 years or so by publication of a number of newly commissioned titles, based on more recent examination of elements of the Petrie Collection by contemporary experts, under the name *Modern Egyptology*. A selection of these additional titles forms the second component of our own series.

The archaeology of Egypt continues to fascinate. Multi-disciplinary investigation and research continues unabated, encompassing methodologies, scientific and data processing techniques, theoretical approaches, and even whole paradigms that were unheard of in the 1970s and undreamt of when Petrie was working in Egypt. Yet all the titles included in this series continue to be invaluable sources of basic data, providing an unparalleled resource that can easily be cross-referenced with the actual materials they describe and discuss. They remain within the Petrie Collection where they may be accessed and re-examined as new research flourishes. As historic documents, the Petrie catalogues stand as exemplars of the craft of typological classification, the backbone of modern archaeology – much of which, though refined by absolute dating and another 100 years of research, still stands the test of time.

A note on presentation

The facsimile titles of Petrie's catalogues re-issued in the 1970s were produced from scans of the original publications. Scanning technology at that time was not of the standard or resolution of today. The scans are no longer available, nor has it been possible to obtain, and in doing so destroy, original copies of the Petrie catalogues. These titles have therefore, of necessity, been rescanned from the 1970s re-issues. Where necessary the pages have been digitally enhanced for clarity of reading and to ensure the good quality of the plates, though inevitably a few are not of the standard we might wish, because of the quality of the previous scan, and occasional blocks of text are not precisely 'straight' or evenly situated on the page. However, some pages in the 1970s re-issues had been inserted in the wrong order and this has been corrected. The originals were produced at a folio size. The pages have been reduced slightly to standard A4 for ease of shelving and because this has the effect of slightly improving the scanned images. In some cases, illustrations were presented to scale and the original scale is given on the plate. There were also no digital files available for titles included in the *Modern Egyptology* series, so these too have been scanned from printed copies.

SHABTIS.

CHAPTER I

SUBSTITUTES FOR THE BODY.

1. Though the funeral statuettes are the commonest of antiquities from Egypt, they have never received more than an incomplete study of certain portions of the whole subject. The most usual form of the inscription was translated by BIRCH (*Z.A.S.* 1864, p. 89, 103; 1865, p. 4, 20); LORET gave an account of the Cairo figures, distinguishing three stages of the inscription, and describing general styles (*Rec.* 1883, p. 89; 1884, p. 70). The inscription has been principally discussed by BORCHARDT (*Z.A.S.* 1894, 111), and GARDINER (*Z.A.S.* 1906, 55). SPELEERS has given a general account of the subject (*Les Figurines Funéraires*), in 1923. With a few other shorter notices, this comprises all that has been collected; there is no systematic registration of details, no collection of all variants of inscription, and translations vary much. I owe to Prof. GUNN many transcriptions from the hieratic.

The material for the present study is mainly the collection which I have gathered at University College, London, of 650 different examples, and the notes of 565 figures in Italian and other museums. Also the copies in the principal publications have been used. This system of registration may help in future publications, and so it is well to suggest the lines of research.

2. When we seek for the starting point of the funeral figures, we pass back stage by stage till we reach the customs of primitive burial in Egypt, so we should begin with that. As soon as the prehistoric burials were recorded, it was noticed that in many instances the bodies had been intentionally dismembered (Naqada), and this has often been noticed since in other cemeteries, extending down to the Vth dynasty (*Deshasheh* 20–24).

Here we are not concerned with the general dismemberment, repeatedly found to have been performed, though the bodies were subsequently entirely wrapped up, bone by bone, and so recomposed (see *Diospolis* 34, *Deshasheh* 20–23, *Meydum* and *Memphis* iv, 19). Our present concern is with the head. It is clear from many instances that the head was removed, probably to be kept apart, and buried later than the body, or sometimes not buried at all in the grave. Among instances in *Naqada*, 30, there is one absolutely unopened grave in which the skull had been put in reversed. In three instances there was a pile of large stones placed in the grave, and the skull placed upright on the top of the pile (*N.* 31). In an intact grave, the skull has been put in reversed (*Diospolis* 32). In two instances necklaces were complete in the graves, once round the neck, and once beneath the skull, yet the skulls had been removed and set upright, one on the spine of the contracted body (*Labyrinth and Gerzeh* 8, 9). Such instances show that besides frequent dismemberment, the skull was specially kept apart, and later added to the body.

3. This custom is what is described in the early funeral ritual of the Pyramid Texts, and the Book of the Dead. We read " Geb has given thee thy head "; " Rise up Teta because thou hast received thy head "; " Nut comes to thee . . . thou movest because she has given thee thy head "; " Pepy Nefer-kara thou hast received thy head." For other extracts, from the Book of the Dead, see Wainwright in *Labyrinth and Gerzeh*, pp. 10–15.

The literary references accord with the actual treatment of the head, as frequently found. This custom seems to be the origin of placing a stone head of the deceased in the shaft of the tomb after the burial of the body (*Ancient Egypt* 1914, 125, and JUNKER). If the actual skull perished, the stone image of the head would remain and be ever ready for the benefit of the deceased (*Ancient Egypt* 1916, 48).

4. It is well known that in West Africa the skull of an ancestor is needed for the benefit of his descendants, enshrined in the house, and receiving offerings at the family meals, in order to ensure the good will of the ancestral spirit (FROBENIUS, *Voice of Africa* 675). Such a primitive habit of thought, still surviving, well explains the purpose of the prehistoric Egyptian in removing the head from the body, and keeping it for some time before restoring it.

The next stage in this custom is to make a model of the head, and to keep it permanently above the tomb, in order to present the offerings before it. In New Calabar an image of the head and shoulders of a chief, or a whole seated figure, is carved in wood and placed on a wooden base or tray, sometimes with smaller images of the sons. The offerings are then laid on the tray before it. This serves as the centre of the daily or weekly worship, of which, as in Egypt, the eldest son is high priest (LEONARD, *Lower Niger* 162—5). Hence we see that the primitive veneration of the ancestral head passes into the veneration of a seated figure, and thus the rise of a system of funeral heads, and finally statues, is actually seen in practice at the present day.

5. Though the burial of a separate head in the tomb, carved in stone, was in use as late as the IVth dynasty, yet entire figures were made before that. The granite figure of the IInd dynasty, found at Memphis (Cairo Mus. 3072) shows the offerer kneeling, evidently in supplication. The inscription reads "He gives an offering, the washer of the high priest of Tehuti, beloved by Tehuti, Dat." The earliest private seated figures, judging by the work, are probably of the IIIrd dynasty, such as the statues at Leyden and Naples (CAPART, *Recueil* ii, iii, li). These have long parted from the natural freshness of the Ist dynasty style, and are not yet influenced by the grand dignity of the IVth dynasty. Rather later, probably about the middle of the IIIrd dynasty, are the standing figures of Sepa and Nes (BISSING, *Denkmäler* 5). The function of these figures to receive offerings is not described in any text of the Old Kingdom, but the festivals are named. The same festivals recur in the prescribed ritual of the tomb of Hepzefa, of the Middle Kingdom, and hence that may be taken as giving a view of the function of the figures. On six great festivals in the year special offerings were made, and on most of them illuminations of the tomb, while on every day there was a loaf and a jug of beer placed before the statue. Such was the material side of the devotion recorded in contracts; but we must read into it the craving for the union with the family spirit, the *ka*, who had been manifest in the ancestor, and was transmitted to his descendants. It was not only the *ka* of the ancestor, but the spirit of the lineage of which he had been the embodiment. On dying, a man went to his *ka*, the *ka* interceded with Ra for the dead, and the offerings were devoted to the *ka*, as being the protector of the dead. Such a dual view accords with modern African beliefs, and reconciles the apparently contradictory statements of the ancients (*Ancient Egypt* 1914, 162).

Inscriptions on the statues only give name and titles. The earliest theological reference is in the Vth dynasty, where the figure is called the *amakhu kher neter oa*, "worthy one before the great God." In the VIth dynasty appears, rarely, the list of royal offerings given for the worthy one, or granted from the royal food-rents due to the king. By the XIIth dynasty this was the constant formula; the royal food-rents are taxed to give an offering to a god, so that the god may provide for the deceased.

In tombs from the IVth dynasty onward, the stone figures were placed for safety in a closed shrine, or *serdab*, and were fed with drink and incense through open slits. In the Xth dynasty tombs of Antaeopolis, the provision of drink was supplied by a long channel which passed under the door of a shrine containing the statue, so as to reach the figure.

CHAPTER II

THE SUBSTITUTE FOR THE MUMMY.

6. In the XIIth dynasty a new style of figure appeared, the beginning of the true ushabti. The downfall of the Old Kingdom system, and the destruction of its tombs, had deeply impressed Egyptian thought, and had shown the futility of trusting to the conservation of the mummy. Now, as physical food could be ensured in perpetuity by models in imperishable stone, it was only a step further to replace the mummy by a stone figure. Such seems to have been the origin of the mummiform figures which begin in the XIIth dynasty. As late as the XIXth dynasty the figure is associated with the bird figure of the *ba*, or soul, as in figs. 98 and 99 here, and the touching figure in Cairo where the *ba* bird waits anxiously to enter the body.

7. In the earlier ages the soul was supposed to reside in the tomb, and to receive the offerings there deposited, and by its statue to benefit from the incense and food continually offered in the tomb chapel. To ensure the protection and comfort of the wandering soul, a model of a hut with food was placed at the side of the grave. It was later amplified as a house fitted with furniture. All this implied that the soul remained on earth; but after the XIIth dynasty a more spiritual theory arose, and it was believed that it belonged to the kingdom of Osiris, Prince of Eternity, Lord of Life. Instead of wandering on earth, dreading to eat dirt, the soul was to go to Osiris, and to be employed in the duties there, as on earth, and to have the pleasures also of its past life. This is familiar to us in the scenes on papyri of the XVIIIth dynasty. In order to perform these duties, hands are needed, and hence the mummy figure with visible hands.

8. The examples of the successive stages of this eschatology are as follows:—

Plain forms without hands, see pls. xxiv–xxvi, XIIth dynasty.
Called a royal offering, nos. 6–39, XVIIth dynasty.
Called a shabti, nos. 40–44, Shauabti 45, XVIIth dynasty.
Wrapped figure with hands, nos. 47, 48.
With tools in the hands, 52, 53, and onward.

9. What appears to be the earliest type of inscription on these figures is that from Hawara, "A royal offering to Osiris lord of Restau that he may grant him (deceased) a coming forth to walk happily in the Duat, that he may behold Ra at his coming forth in the horizon." From the fine work, this is of the XIIth dynasty but, by its source, not before Amenemhat III. Another figure of the same age is inscribed "A royal offering to Osiris, lord of Zedu, that he may grant an oratory, food, and drink, for the *ka* of the lady of the house Hent-nefert" (figures, *Labyrinth* xxx). Another figure, of the same form, reads "Made by favour of the king for the keeper of the great house of the king, Amenqen (*Cem. Abyd.* II, xxxix 5). The type without arms or hands was also made later, as no. 49 under Tehutmes III, but it is rare. The type with arms also begins in the Middle Kingdom, as "Royal offering to Osiris for the *ka* of the Intendant of the North Land (Delta) Nekht," and of a priest Nekhta (*Arabeh* iii, vi).

10. It should be noted that MARIETTE attributed to the XIIth and XIIIth dynasties many ushabtis of a later style, and this has been followed by LORET and others. The texts on these are not of XIIth but of XVIIIth type. The absence of legs to animal hieroglyphs is not a proof of early age, as it occurs as late as the XXth dynasty (L.D. III 235–6), and on an ushabti at Florence of Aohmes praiser of Amen. Another reputedly XIIth dynasty ushabti of Ren-senb (*Cem. Abyd.* II, 113) omits *nesut da hetep* and has the vocative before "ushabti," and the phrase *aptu*, and the sowing and watering clauses, all of the XVIIIth or later. Whether this is the Ransenb of Tehutmes I (*Arabeh* xxii) is uncertain, as GARSTANG supplied no numbers and PEET made no plan, so the two accounts are unconnected. Another ushabti reputed to give the early text (Anhurmes in *Arabeh* 35) has the word *am* before clause 28, which is unknown till XXIst dynasty, and the smiting clause, 22, which is not early. It is of the type of the revival in XXVth dynasty, like Harua and no. 545 in vertical columns.

It seems, then, that by the close of the Middle Kingdom the duplicate figure of the mummy had been provided with arms and hands in order to act, and that it was generally inscribed with the royal offering formula for the *ka* of the deceased. At this point we lose sight of it in the gloom of the Hyksos age until it reappears, further developed, in the XVIIth dynasty.

CHAPTER III

THE GROWTH OF THE SHUABTI.

11. Of recent years a large number of figures have been found at Thebes, which are evidently from a family cemetery, shortly before the XVIIIth dynasty. The only description at first hand is by NEWBERRY in *Excavations in the Theban Necropolis.* Scattered ones have come through dealers to the British Museum, and at Thebes I bought about forty.

They are closely linked in formula to the stone figures already described, all of mummy form without hands; but in the intervening centuries there was an enormous degradation. These are all of wood, roughly split and chopped, and some even show no difference between head and feet. Yet they retain the old formula, and represent mummies, as many of them have model coffins, see nos. 3, 3 A, 39 A, pls. xxiv, xxv. Some had a model tomb also (*N.T.N.* 27).

Most of these bore the royal offering formula in rude hieroglyphics, but later ones have the ushabti formula in hieratic. There are 59 royal offerings, and 21 shuabtis at that date. The royal offering text, or plain names, are on nos. 5 to 46, transcribed on pls. vi, vii. Several have the provider's name, his mother or brother, "to cause his name to live." This does not therefore refer to the posterity continuing to live, but the name of the deceased living when called to serve in the kingdom of Osiris.

12. The god to whom the royal offering is made is Osiris on 34, Ptah on 5, Seker on 4 examples. The position of Ptah, as god of the dead, is notable at Thebes. The compounding of the gods is shown by the singular *daf*, or the plural *da-sen*. Ptah and Seker once remain separate, but otherwise united as Ptah-Seker-Osiris, or Ptah-Osiris. The formation of composite gods was just in progress at this age, and this implies the complete fusion of the different stocks of worshippers, perhaps due to the pressure of the Hyksos.

13. The group from 5 to 28 is entirely of one family of six brothers, sons of Antef and Săt-art. The successive deaths are traced by the names of the dedicators,

for the son Antef by Teta-nefer (12)
for Teta-nefer by Teta-mes (19) and Teta-onkh (18)
for Teta by Teta-mes (10) and Teta-onkh (17)
for Teta-on by Teta-onkh (24)

Other royal offering formulas are on 31 to 39, and the shuabti formula on 40 to 45, all cursive hieratic.

14. At this point, in view of the mere scraps of wood which were to do all that the deceased could do in the underworld, we may well turn to an account which is a satire on this belief, as it still existed in Greek times. It is so entirely foreign to western magic that it is evidently a parody true to its surroundings. Lucian, in his dialogue on lying, gives a story by Eucrates as follows:—

"While I resided in Egypt, whither I was sent very young by my father, for the purposes of study, I conceived a desire to go up the Nile to Coptos for the sake of hearing Memnon, who at sunrise utters such surprising tones. (Coptos being the garrison town would be headquarters for a trip to Thebes.) I did hear him; not as the generality do, yielding a bare sound without meaning, but I heard a real oracle out of Memnon's own mouth, in seven verses ... On our return there happened to be in the same ship with me a man of Memphis, ... of the sacred order, with a shaven crown, dressed entirely in linen, always absorbed in meditation, speaking very pure Greek, a tall man, lean, with a pendulous under-lip, and somewhat spindle-shanked ... When I saw him, as often as we went on shore, among other surprising feats, ride upon crocodiles, and swim about among these and other aquatic animals, and perceived what respect they had for him by wagging their tails, I concluded that the man was holy, and sought to ingratiate myself with him that he might communicate to me his secrets. At length he persuaded me to leave my slaves at Memphis, and to follow him alone, telling me that we should not lack for servants. When we came to an inn, he would take the wooden bar of the door, or a broom, or the pestle of a mortar, put clothes on it, and speaking over it a magical formula, made it walk, and be taken by everybody for a man. This servant went to draw water for us, did the cooking, arranged the furniture, and showed itself in every respect an intelligent and active servant. Then when Pancrates no longer needed it, by a second enchantment it became a broom if it had been a broom, a pestle if it had been a pestle ... One day hiding myself in a dark corner, I heard, unknown to him, the magic formula. It was a word of three syllables ...

Next day when my Egyptian was occupied in the market place I took the pestle, I dressed it, and pronounced the three magic syllables and ordered it to go and fetch water. It brought me an amphora full. 'Enough,' I said, 'do not bring more water, become again a pestle.' But it would not obey me, it continued bringing water, and filled all the house. I knew not what to do. I feared Pancrates would be angry on his return, as he was when he did come. I seized an axe and split the pestle in two. Immediately each piece of wood took an amphora and went to fill it with water, so that in place of one servant I had two. At this point Pancrates returned, guessed at once what had happened, and turned again to wood my two water carriers, as they were before the enchantment. But some days afterwards he left me without my knowing it, and I have not known since what has become of him."

Now whether this was borrowed directly from the belief in the shuabti or no, the magic ideas are closely the same. A shapeless piece of wood, like these early shuabtis, can by a magic formula be made to do all the work of a man; and even if split in two, as rudely as these shabtis are split, each piece will continue to have the same magic powers. Perhaps the word of three syllables referred to was Sha-uab-ti, as that is the word first uttered in conjuring the figures to do the work. This story has been revived in modern times in a French symphonic poem.

15. Various sources for the word *Shuabti* have been proposed. *Shau* to be useful, or serve, or appointment, or fitness (*sha* to appoint). *Uab* satisfaction, contenting, *uabti* he who is satisfied. *Usheb* to answer; but the figure is never commanded "*usheb*," but "*ka*," in reply. *Shuab* is the persea tree, but no figures of that wood are known. *Usheb* means also to eat or nourish, *Ushabti* nourisher, but the work was weaving or shifting sand, not providing food.

CHAPTER IV

GROWTH OF THE SHUABTI FORMULA.

16. The simplest type of formula, found on the earliest class of figure bearing the name of *shuabti*, is merely "O shabti of Sen-hetep, made by his brother making his name to live Aoh-hetep" (42). "Shauabti this, Aoh-mes Sa-pa-(ar)" (45). "O shauabti Sa-pa-art" (44). These simply assert that the figure in some way belongs to the deceased. A further step is to call it "shabti for the *ka* of Să-ra" (43). Thus the shabti is to act for the family spirit (see sect. 43, pls. vi, vii, xxiv–xxvi).

17. In only two instances do we find the royal offering formula associated with the shabti formula. This indicates a very brief overlap of the two formulae; when the shabti formula was once started, it was soon the only one accepted. No. 18 of NEWBERRY reads "Royal offering to Osiris lord of Zedu, great god, lord of Abydos, may he give an oratory, oxen, geese, clothing, incense, ointment ... for the *ka* of N... made by his mother who makes his name to live, M... Shabti, if one calls for me (to carry) sands of west to east, 'Behold me' reply thou." No. 19 of NEWBERRY gives a longer form, after the royal offering. "O Shabti this, if one summons thee in the west or in the east to carry sand or water, to weave clothes, then (reply) thou to Osiris 'I am doing it behold me' reply thou to him."

18. We next find the formula lengthened by a repetition, before being amplified by more subjects. The duplicated formulae are no. 28 *N.T.N.*, "Shuabti this, Aohmes, if one summons thee to all work in Kher-neter, 'I am doing' say thou, as a servant; if summoned to fill channels, or sand from east to west, 'I am doing' say thou." No. 32 *N.T.N.* is rather longer, "O Shauabuti this, if one is going to send in the name of Nefer-hetep, to carry sand of west to east, say thou 'Behold I am doing, behold me'; if summoned in the name of Nefer-hetep to works, say thou, repeat thou to him, 'Done' to him." For the general view of all this, and following inscriptions, see the tables pls. i–iv, and the general table of formula growth, pl. v.

19. The next idea that comes in is the reckoning of the workers; the work is to be not merely a casual order to be done when called for, but a numbering—*ap*—of the workers, counting them up. The hieratic shabti U.C. 41 reads "Shauabti this, if one calls and numbers such an one to do all works there in Kher-neter, 'Behold me' say thou." The same, rather fuller, appears for Teta-res (*Z.A.S.* xxxii, 113) "Shabti this, Teta-res, if is numbered Teta-res to do all works that are to be done in Kher-neter, to make grow the fields, to fill the channels, to produce ... to transport sand of the east to the west 'Behold me' say thou." This is the first extension of the formula to field cultivation, and there was also added the clause "to produce" (*sekheper*, something erased), which never occurs again. The details were still quite variable, and not yet crystallized. It is to be observed that the shabti is still called by the name of the man, Teta-res; it is to be identical with him in all claims for working.

20. The next new clause appears in the figure of Teta-on (*N.T.N.* 22), and best, perhaps, on that of Qed-hetep (*Arabah* xv). The latter reads "O shauabti this, if one numbers Qed-hetep in all works to be done in Kher-neter, as a man at his business, to cause to grow the fields, to cause to fill the channels, to transport the sand of the east to the west, 'I am doing it Behold me,' say thou." The new clause that the work is to be done "as a man at his business" is obscure, probably owing to its colloquialism; the "business," *kheriu*, means anything that is put under a man, within his power or control. RENOUF renders it as "abilities," LORET as "condition," we might also say work on subjects that he can do, or affairs. We should try to grasp this in its form here, because soon after it becomes mixed up with another clause which complicates it. It might be paraphrased, "if the deceased is levied to do work of the kind of work that he understands and can perform."

21. At this point of development come in two new features, the title of Osiris for the deceased, and the phrase *sehez*. Before both become generally used together, there are noted 9 with *sehez* alone, and 5 Osiris alone; but each term was occasionally used alone in later times. The priority is settled by those with Osiris alone being of the rude style of figure, while those with *sehez* alone are of fine work. This shows that Osiris was of earlier introduction, but was not regularly used till after Nehi the viceroy of Tehutmes III. The earliest Osiride formulae (*N.T.N.* 30, 29) are "This Osiris Tetamesu. O Shauabti 'I am doing it, behold me with thee' (say) as one calls thee because of carrying from west to east"; also of the same man, "O Shauab this, if one numbers Osiris Tetamesu to all works to be done in Kher-neter, to cause to grow the fields (to cause to fill the channels), to transport the sand of the west to the east, 'I am doing it, behold me,' say thou." This shows that the assertion of the shauabti being the man in question continued until the man was Osirified, whatever that may mean; but evidently the codeifying of the man must result in a separation between him and the figure which is to be ordered by Osiris. The Osiris title is the first occurrence of regarding the shabti as a slave, though a sign of that appears, probably earlier, on the figure of Aohmes (*N.T.N.* 28) where the shuabti is to reply "like a servant."

22. The meaning of the term *sehez*, which became universally applied to shabtis, is not yet settled. It means not only to make physically bright, but also to explain or interpret writings, as in our phrase "illuminating." It even becomes used for an overseer, *sehez per* being translated "overseer of the palace," the man who "brightened up" the place, as we say. It is by no means always joined with the Osiris title, often it is applied directly to the name of the man and, in one instance at least, to the shabti. ("*Sehez* shabti this of Osiris Tetanefer born of Baka," &c. *Z.A.S.* 1894, 115). It is certainly not an adjective, as it precedes the subject. It becomes universal in shabtis; it is rare, or unknown, on steles or other places. Hence it appears to be an order or declaration connected with the shabti, and seems likely to be connected with the instruction by the deceased to the shabti.

The earliest dated formula of this type is of Senemaoh (47), under Tehutmes I, and this is identical with the figure of Nehi (48) governor of the Sudan under Tehutmes III, which may be taken as the finest work, and most complete type, of the early *sehez* form:—"Make clear, royal son of the land of the south, Nehi, *maot kheru*. He says, O Shuabti this, if one numbers the royal son of the land of the south, Nehi, in works to be done there in Kher-neter as a man at his business, to cause to grow the fields, to cause to fill the channels, to transport sands of east to west, 'Behold me' say thou."

23. With the coming in of the complete formula *sehez Asar*, is also another phrase unknown before, *ar heseb tu*, "if one reckons." The figure of Userhot (U.C. 52) shows the beginning of a new order of things. All the earlier figures were simply mummy figures or had hands shown, but at this point there appears a hoe in each hand and a bag at each side. The details of shabti tools are dealt with later (sect. 37, pl. xiv), but here we note that the radical change takes place with the later style of ribbed wig, the *sehez asar* formula, and the phrase of reckoning. The inscription of Userhot is "make clear, Osiris, scribe of the troops of the lord of two lands, Userhot; he says, O Shabti this, if one numbers, if one reckons in (all) works to be done in Kher-neter, as a man at his business ..." (the remainder is lost). A rare link with the past is the early formula of a royal offering in a column down the back of the figure.

24. The next stage is the introduction of the clause about smiting evils. This is usually joined to the clause "there as a man at his business," but not always so; the other connection of it helps to show the sense. The smiting is to be by, or for, "him if numbered at any time." Now, the whole structure of the inscription is based on the following type:—"Says *he* to the Shabti, if N. is called to work, to carry sand, then one smites for *him* evils." Him, *f*, cannot here refer to the shabti, but to the person who is directing the shabti, and who is called on to work. Hence it cannot read "then shall he strike down evil," because the person is supposed to be quiescent. The sense therefore seems to limit the meaning, by the various contexts. Clauses that are sometimes omitted are here in [ ] and explanations in ( ), as follows:—In the

XVIIIth dynasty the person says, if he is called on to carry sand, "then thou (the shabti) shalt smite for him (the person) evils as a man at his business if numbered at any time,"—that is, to act as a body guard. In the XXVIth dynasty the person says, if called on to work in Kher-neter, "then thou (shabti) shalt smite for him (person) evils as a man at his business (thoroughly), Behold me, reply ye, if numbered at any time to work there, to cause to grow the fields," &c. Thus when the person is called to work, the shabti is to work for him, and to protect the person.

The royal figure of Amenhetep II, no. 65 (see inscrip. pl. ix, 65) differs from private ushabtis in nature, not being called an ushabti. It reads, "make clear, king Oa-khepru-ra *maot kheru*; he says O, these (statuettes) of the eternal prince Amenhetep, *neter heq an*, if it is ordained, if one numbers, to do all works that are to be done in Kher-neter, then smite thou as a man at his business; behold say thou *maot kheru*."

25. During the XVIIIth dynasty the formula was by no means crystallized, but it fluctuated somewhat in order, and by new sentences added at the writer's discretion. This is seen, in the comparative table of texts, by the quantity of exceptions at this period. We shall here note the exceptional sentences in the order in which they occur in the standard text. The context of the standard is in ( ).

Between clauses 12 and 18 "(If one numbers, if one reckons) if I am sought at any time (to do all works, &c.)" (Cairo, no. 75, LORET).

Between 16 and 29 "(If thou art summoned, Aohmes) there go (to cause to fill the channels)" (*N.T.N.* 20).

Between 17 and 29 "(If one numbers, if one reckons, the Osiris Ra-user in Kher-neter) saying be strong with the hoe in the pools (to cause to fill the channels)" (*M.C.A.* 427). This gives the name for the hoe usually figured on the shabti, *aken-nu*.

After 22 "(thou shalt smite for him evils, as a man at his business) if thou art summoned daily" (Amenmes, U.C. 60).

After 28 "(to cause to grow the fields) united with its people." That is to say, along with the other serfs of the field.

After 29 "(to cause to fill the channels) who art of the court of servants." See nameless figure, *M.C.A.* 431.

Between 29 and 35 "(to cause to fill the channels), to do all messages to be done in Kher-neter. 'I am doing, behold me' reply thou in the condition of one carrying. The Osiris Bakenamen is harboured in peace at Amenti as chief of a city" (Cairo 97, LORET).

After 33 "(as a man in his business, to be numbered at any time) as thou repeatest well 'Me, behold,' reply likewise (ye) who daily for ever repeat (this)." Upuat-mes (Leiden, *Mon.* II, iii).

After 38 "(behold me reply thou) there; listen thou to him who made thee, do not listen to his enemies, as one calls thee because of carrying from west to east, (say) 'I am doing, behold me, with thee'" (Berlin, *Z.A.S.* 1895, 119).

After 38 "(reply thou) there in Kher-neter." Any (*R.M.A.* xli).

After 38 "(reply thou) there in the hour when following Unnefer, great god, prince of eternity." Tau (*M.C.A.* 425).

After 38 "(reply thou) if reckoned at any time in the business of every day." Ptahmes (*M.C.A.* 408).

After 38 (carrying sand) "if one calls, if I am sought in the timing of every day, I am doing, behold me." Neny (Leiden, *Mon.* II, x).

After 32 (carrying sand) "if I am sought at any time at all." Mehy-hetep (U.C. 106).

The figure of Huy (Leiden, *Mon.* xv) may be accepted as the most perfect text of the XVIIIth to XIXth dynasty. It reads "Make clear, Osiris . . . Huy, He says O shuabti this if one numbers, if one reckons, the Osiris Huy to do all works to be done in Kher-neter, to cause to grow the fields, to cause to fill the channels, to transport the sand from east to west there, as a man at his business, smite for him evils there; if numbered at any time 'I am doing, behold me' say."

26. At the close of the XVIIIth dynasty there arises in the inscription the greater frequency of the clause "if numbered to work at every day" or "continually." This change was assigned by LORET as distinctive of his second version, in which he also included the change of the middle XVIIIth dynasty, introducing the clause of smiting evil. Indeed, it is not clear which of these changes he means when naming the second text. He places the beginning of the second text to Amenhetep III in three instances, Heq-er-neheh, Thuaă, and a sarcophagus; and among the seven shabtis of Thunure (Cairo 32) there is one of the first text, and the rest are of the second. In no clause is there at all the clean division of date between a first, second and third text, such as has been assumed by various writers. The only statement that can cover the facts, is to date the order of introduction of the single clauses, and their period when possible, as we are doing here. The greater frequence of the continued work is associated with the conception of the figures as slaves, rather than as doubles of the deceased person. With this arises the idea of needing task masters, dressed in a waist-cloth and carrying a whip; the earliest of such figures belongs probably to the age of Sety I, as we shall notice further on. The shabtis of the XIXth to XXVth dynasties show a continual shortening and corruption of the inscriptions. The only distinct change is that the clause of "smiting evil thoroughly" begins to be placed before instead of after the triple field works, probably starting there in the XIXth dynasty (Ptahmes inlaid glaze, Cairo) and never found placed after the field works later than the XXth dynasty (Rameses IV).

27. The last great change in the history of the text was the establishment of a long standard edition at the beginning of the XXVIth dynasty, after which the only variation is shortening by omission. This new text was beginning about 690 B.C. as shown by the figures of Amenardas (U.C. 535–8) and her high steward Herua (540); to this class belong the figures of Nesiptah (534) and Anhurmes (542) which have no back pillar. Nesiptah has a beard, while the more completely inscribed Pedu-amenapt has none, showing an overlap of customary form. The next stage is that Shepenapt II, perhaps 650 B.C. has the introductory clauses with the name, but not the fullest text of Peduamenapt. This latter noble has left many shabtis, now all broken, disunited and scattered among many museums; they are of brown serpentine, of the finest engraving and the most complete text known. They serve as the standard text for all later time, and read thus:—"Make clear, Osiris, chief reciter, Pedu-amenapt; He says O Shabti this, if one calls, if one numbers, if one reckons, the Osiris, chief reciter, Peduamenapt to do all works that are to be done there in Kher-neter, then thou shalt smite evils there, as a man at his business; 'Behold him' say thou if one numbers at any time, to be done (act) there, to cause to grow the fields, to cause to fill the channels, to transport the sands of the west to east, and *vice-versa*, 'Behold me' say thou if one seeks the Osiris, chief reciter, Peduamenapt, 'I am doing it, behold me' say thou." After this, there are no further changes except degradation, until the latest text appears at the end of the XXXth dynasty. For royal shabtis, the text was kept up almost to standard form until the last native king Nekht-her-heb.

CHAPTER V

OTHER TEXTS ON SHUABTIS.

28. Various other texts occasionally appear inscribed on the figures. The earliest such is on three rough wooden figures of the XVIIth dynasty (*N.T.N.* XX, 24–26). Prof. NEWBERRY's translation is much cleared by the relationships of the persons given by their shabtis already described, sect. 13. The person named Teta-res is probably the same as Teta-on, being written with the same eye sign, but with different spelling. Teta-nefer and Teta-on were brothers according to the relations shown by the shabtis, and Teta-nefer died before Teta-on. We can read the inscriptions in view of these facts. Explanations are in ( ).

No. 26. "O Teta-res wander to seek Teta-nefer (who died before) go around if (thy shabti) is bringing for thee sand." That is to say, he was to seek his elder brother and help him with his shabtis' share of carrying sand.

No. 24. "Royal offering to Osiris (lord of) Zedu, may he give an oratory, oxen and geese, for the *ka* of Teta-res (son of) Antef. (Message) Teta-res wander to seek and he will be found (Teta-nefer)."

No. 25. "Pa-medu wander to seek Teta-res, that he may call by name to the *ka* of Teta-nefer. If you are told to carry sand of west to east 'I go' say." Here a servant, Pa-medu, is told to seek Teta-res to give him a message for the guardian *ka* of Teta-nefer, and to accept orders from him to work.

These are very interesting, as messages given at burial to the corpse to be delivered to those previously deceased. This implies more of the interaction of the deceased than is generally supposed. The messages belong to the earliest period of the Theban royal wooden figures, as the family only use the royal offering formula, and never the word *shauabti*. These injunctions remind us of the old Scotch woman who was told, when dying, to take various messages, and replied "Hoot awa, ye dinna think I'll gae clack-clacking thro' hēven looking for your folk."

Another early formula (*N.T.N.* 15) resembles that of the oldest mummiform figure, desiring a coming forth in the Duat; it reads "Royal offering given to Osiris, great god, lord of Abydos, that he may give things good and pure, and entering and going forth in Restau, for the *ka* of Mesu." Restau, now Resht, was the port of Aalu on the Caspian Sea.

29. A formula of the time of Amenhetep III (Cairo, 50 LORET) names both Anubis and the Aten. It reads, "Royal offering to Anpu who is in the temple, the great god, lord of Amenti, that he may give a glorious coming forth to behold the Aten, to breathe the sweet wind of the north, for the *ka* of the Osiris greatly favoured by the good god."

The standard text of the orthodox Aten worshippers is given by two figures: C is one in Cairo (*Musée Egyptien* III, 27) and Z is one in Zurich (*P.S.B.A.* 1885, p. 202). These are identical except in the passages in [ ]. They read,—"Royal offering given to the living Aten who makes bright the earth with his beauties, may he give sweet wind of the north, a long duration of life in the excellent Amenti, C. gifts cool water, wine, milk, on the table of offerings of his tomb, C. [gifts of all young flowers, Z.] for the *ka* of the lieutenant Hot, C. [his sister, lady of the house, Qedet, Z.]" These figures are not at all alike, the Cairo one is of most exquisite carving of wood, that at Zurich of brown pottery; hence the text must have been general, because carved by artists in different materials.

30. Early in the XIXth dynasty, another formula is found (Leiden, *Mon.* II, xvi). "Royal offering given to Osiris Khent-amenti, to Ptah-seker lord of the *shethy* (shrine), to Anpu within the temple, that they may give an entering and going forth into Kher-neter, breathing sweet wind of the north, taking bread forth before the roll of rations of the lord of Ta-zeser, following Seker in Restau and Osiris in Zedu, and a good burial for the future, in the western temple of Memphis (DE ROUGÉ, *Geog.* 4), for the chief of the Memphite palace of the lord of the lands, Aohmes." Down the front of the dress, in one column, is "A forthcoming of everything upon their table of all things good and pure." This is parallel to the inscription on the front of the dress of Khoemuas (U.C. 99), "A forthcoming upon the table before the lord of Ta-zeser, for the king's son Khoemuas."

31. A form rarely found, in the XVIIIth dynasty, was to state that the figure was given in honour (praises), *du em hesu*, of the man. A fine example here is U.C. 49, "Given in honour from the king for the praised (dead), who greatly filled the heart of the lord of both lands, child of the harym (*kep*), chief of the archers of Zaru, keeper of the horses, Monuna." The title *khred ne kep*, here rendered "child of the harym," occurs on other shabtis, as Senb (Cairo, *M.C.A.* 385), Mentu, Arab, and Amenmes (all Bologna) with the house determinative. Another such formula is *Du em hesu nt kher nesut*, "given in honour from the king, for the keeper of the cattle, fan bearer, Amen-qen" (Cairo, 45 LORET).

32. The idea of personal service was developed from the XIXth dynasty onward. Even in the beginning of the XVIIIth dynasty, there is the injunction to act as a servant. Early in the XIXth there are figures of the deceased High Priest Ptahmes, grinding corn, inscribed "I am the servant of this god, his grinder." But this was a substitute or servant, not the person, as another inscription reads, "Says he I am the grinder of Osiris, servant of Nut, for the *ka* of the guardian of the treasury, Mery-mery" or Mery-y. The purpose of these figures is essentially different from the old figures of domestics of the VIth to XIIth dynasties; these are to work for the gods in lieu of the noble, the older figures were slaves to work for the noble himself. These belong to the heavenly kingdom of Osiris; the others belonged to the life of the dead on earth (*Z.A.S.* 1906, 55). The idea of a substitute being a servant grew in the XIXth dynasty, until one figure is inscribed "Servant of Tauekhed" (*Z.A.S.* 1911, 127). Yet even here the figure has the long full wig of the lady herself, and is therefore intended to personate her, although called a servant.

33. In the XIXth dynasty a new opening to the formula was sometimes used, "Speech made by the Osiris N., says he O Shabti, &c." (*Z.A.S.* 1905, 81). Here the word "speech" stands in place of *sehez*; this confirms the meaning of *sehez*, preceding the address to the shabti.

Very short formulae occur on the figures of Zedptah-auf-onkh of the XXIInd dynasty; on some "I am Z., behold thou"; others "I am the follower in Amenti" or "in Duat," or the follower of Osiris (*Rec.* V, 70). These seem to show at that time a weakening in the idea of service to Osiris, and there only remained the intention of providing a substitute for the mummy to follow the gods.

The latest appearance of some formulae may be noted here. The royal offering occurs in the middle of the XVIIIth dynasty (Hor, Cairo 43, 61, and Huta 68) and in the XIXth (U.C. from Rifeh). *Ne ka ne* occurs on two figures of the XIXth dynasty (Bologna, U.C. 233). *Amakh*, after the early XVIIIth dynasty, was revived in the XXVIth. *O shabti* after the early XVIIIth, was revived in the XXVth, XXVIth and XXXth dynasties.

34. Various questions regarding the usual formula do not seem to have had enough consideration. The nature of the work which Osiris would require of the deceased, and which was passed on to the shabti, is an essential matter. What appears to be the earliest requirement is the weaving of clothing, next the carrying of sand, then irrigation, and the last claim was for making the fields grow. The provision of tools does not appear till some generations later than the demand for works. It seems that the subjects of Osiris were to take part in an organized society, doing all the needful business of life, and not only agriculture. What then is the meaning of carrying the sand of the east to the west? In the cultivation of Egypt, as we know of it, there is no great carrying of sand. It has been suggested that it might refer to taking the *sebakh* dust from the towns bordering the Nile on the rocky eastern side, across to the broad cultivated plain on the western side. Although in two of the earliest texts, and some later ones, the word for carry is *fat*, which might mean by land or by water, yet the regular word here is *kheny* "to row," and the determinative of a boat is added. This strongly shows that the sand had to be moved across the water from east to west. The difficulty in supposing this to refer to *sebakh* is that there is no evidence that the town dust was utilised anciently as a fertiliser. If used as at present, some reference would surely be found to the interminable details of farm life in contracts on Roman papyri. It was used before 1800 A.D. as the ruins of Bubastis are shown dug out, in the French views of the *Description*; no high house walls could remain bare for centuries, in the Delta, without being weathered down flat. Also no trace of ancient digging over sites has been observed during modern excavations; town mounds of all ages still stand in their original strata and levels. It seems quite impossible that an extensive system of *sebakh* digging was a main labour in Egypt when the shabti instructions were framed. Again, it is questionable if town dust would be called *sho*, sand. The only labour in moving sand that we can imagine would be shifting back the sand dunes which encroached on the cultivated land. In parts of the western edge of the Nile valley, high sand dunes slowly march forward and extinguish the fields; in one district, half a dozen ridges of dunes, about a furlong apart, line the valley edge, with grassy plains low enough to be inundated lying between them. Such masses, twenty to forty feet in height, could hardly be shifted by man, yet in other districts (as Saqqareh) low rolls of sand a foot or two high encroach on the cultivation. Where a water channel bordered the western edge (as it usually did, owing to that being lower than the rest of the alluvial plain), then shifting the sand by boat across from the fields to the desert, from east to west, might have been worth undertaking. This seems to be the least improbable sense of the instruction.

For references from the photographs of ushabtis to the text, first look in Chapter vii, transliterations, for the name corresponding to the number of the photograph. Refer the name to the alphabetical list of names, pls. xvi–xxiii: this will give the titles, name, and parentage, the form, material, arrangement and type of formula, also the museum reference, according to pl. xv. Next refer the number to the facsimile copy in pls. vi to xiv. The list of names and titles, xvi–xxiii, gives a catalogue of the shabtis of Bologna, British Museum, Cairo, Florence, Leyden, Naples, Collegio Romano, Turin, Vatican, as well as those in University College, London.

CHAPTER VI

FORM AND MATERIALS OF SHUABTIS.

35. The history of the form of the shabti should be considered with reference to the types of names associated with the forms. There is no published list of names giving the range of date of each, and therefore we need first to gain some idea of the changing fashions in names. The political importance of different centres brought certain gods into prominence at one time or another, and this is reflected in the devotion to those gods. But more important is the form of devotion. The child is ascribed to divine favour, as Amenhetep "Amen contents," or Erdune-ptah, "Ptah gave"; in later times dedication to a god is more usual, as Pen amen, "This is for Amen," Bak-ne-khensu, "Servant of Khonsu," Nesiptah "He who belongs to Ptah," Pedu amen "The gift of Amen." Here we can only notice a few of the limits of age of certain forms of name which help in dating the shabtis. Names with *nekht* begin as early as the XIIth dynasty, see Amen-nekht (LIEB. *Dict.* 114) and Sebek-nekht (Scarab 12 E). Amen-nekht and Sebek-nekht occur under Amenhetep III, but the main period of the name was in the XIXth dynasty. Penaati occurs under Tehutmes III, and Penanher had a sister Hat-sheps (LIEB. 437), though the type of name was far commoner in the XIXth dynasty. Bak-names begin in the XVIIIth dynasty, as Baken-khensu who was high priest under Amenhetep III. Nesi was used in names of the Old Kingdom, as Nesemnau; in the Middle Kingdom, Nesonkh-senbef, and Nessu. The earliest of the frequent *nesi*-names seems to have been given under Ramessu about 1140 B.C., Nesi-ba-neb-zedu of Tanis; a generation later the use of *nesi-* spread to Thebes, in the name Nesi-khensu. The form Pedu- first appears with Pedu-bast high priest under Ramessu III. The form Zed- is probably as early as the XIXth dynasty, in Zed-ne-skhoba-ast (LIEB. 975), but began to be usual with Zed-khensu-auf-onkh son of Panezem II. All of these points serve to show the limits of different classes of shabtis.

36. The figures with hands but without any tools are a sixth of the whole; they were usual for royal persons, as Sety I, Ramessu III and VI, Amenardus and Shepenapt. Of private persons with hands empty, the names are nearly all of the XVIIIth dynasty style, and the latest are three Ramessu names. One Zed-khensu is copied from the Vatican; in the glass cases the details are not seen, so the tools could not always be recorded. The purely mummy figure without tools ceases with the XVIIIth dynasty, except in royal persons or rare examples of private persons. The beginning of the representation of tools is more difficult to define, as the personal name does not entirely prove the date, for names tend to drag on. Of those here, User-hot (52) is probably the earliest and, from the style of work, apparently between Tehutmes III and Amenhetep III. The bronze figure of Any, found buried on the road to the shrine of Osiris at Abydos, has no tools in the hands, but model tools were buried with it. This I should attribute to Tehutmes III. It seems, then, as if the idea of the figures being fitted out for their work began after the great importation of slaves from the Asiatic wars of Tehutmes III, and became universal about 150 years later. One of the early stages of tools was when a shabti was buried in a model coffin with wooden models of hoes, buckets and yoke, and brick mould, apparently to make bricks rather than to do cultivation (*El Amrah* xxxix). The tools were otherwise of bronze, inscribed with the owner's name, as a model bag (*El Amrah* xxxviii, xl) and model axe, chisels and hoes (*El Amrah* xlv).

37. The hoes are at first of two forms, broad and narrow (see 66 and pl. xiv); later they are usually only narrow. In the XXVIth dynasty a pick with a short blade is always shown with the narrow hoe. This pick always has the blade tang inserted through the wooden handle (see 547 and 551, 553, pl. xiv).

The provision of water pots and yokes (see 113 and 112, pl. xiv) is less common, being only placed on about one in thirty. They are probably all of the time of Ramessu II, as not one of the twenty-four names need lie beyond that reign.

The baskets or bags were at first carried in the hands with the hoes (see 63, 66), but the position on the back hung over the shoulder became general (see 113 and pl. xiv). From the form and size they are for carrying seed, not earth.

38. The figures of overseers with a kilt begin in the XIXth dynasty, not a single name shows an earlier date. The earliest class (XV 52, see nos. 94, 100) is that with folded arms. The same is true of the class XV 58 with two hoes, and the type with 60 (see no. 85) *thet* and *zed* in the hands. The later classes (54, 56) are those with the whip in one hand, and the other arm down the side; these begin with the XIXth dynasty, as the beautiful Hor (here no. 253) belongs almost to the Akhenaten glazes, and the latest of this style with whip in right hand are of the XXIst dynasty, and with whip in left hand, of the XXIInd dynasty. The two figures with long robe are for Panezem I, XXIst, and Zed-bast-auf-onkh (477) probably of XXIInd dynasty. The overseer figures continue in very rude form, without names, down to the end of the XXIIIrd dynasty, but they are never found in the revived style of the XXVth dynasty and onward.

39. Regarding materials, the stone figures of the Middle Kingdom were usually of fine hard white limestone, or of dark brown serpentine. Wood rarely appears then; but it became the only material in the dark ages, as we find in the rude figures of the XVIIth dynasty. It was used for the finest work, as of Nehi (43) under Tehutmes III, and Thay (73), and it continued usual throughout the XIXth dynasty. Some very rude figures, perhaps of the XXIInd dynasty, are covered with green colour-wash, like the mud figures, to imitate glaze. After that it seems never to have been used.

The next material employed was soft limestone, as in the figure of Sen-em-aoh (47) under Tehutmes I, and this continued in common use till the XIXth dynasty. After that it only appears rarely in the XXVth dynasty, as Anhermes (542). A black limestone came into use, perhaps first for the figures of Amenhetep II; fine work in this material is seen in the figures of Min-mes (66), Sadiamia (68) and Mutnezem (Brit. Mus.). An easy imitation of this was the black steatite as in Mehy-nef (69) and Ta-neb-nefert (70). The use of this in the XIXth dynasty is seen in the figure of Kho-em-uas (99) and another (100), and the fine bust of that age (101). It does not appear to have been used later than Ramessu II.

Alabaster was occasionally used from the late XVIIIth to the XXth dynasty. Probably it was started by the alabaster carving of Akhenaten's age; though the names do not appear to be earlier than the XIXth dynasty. The end of it (as 249) was in the very rude pegs of stone, daubed with red and green wax, for Ramessu VI.

Serpentine, brown or green, was adopted in the revival of the XXVth dynasty, by Amenardus, Harua, Peduamenapt and Shepenapt.

Sandstone rarely appears, plain or painted, and only early in the XIXth dynasty. Red granite was used for the figures of Amenhetep III and Akhenaten; grey granite was used for Amenemant, in the XIXth dynasty.

Bronze very rarely appears, as for Any (under Tehutmes III? Brit. Mus.), Ramessu II (Louvre), and Ramessu III (Cairo).

40. Red pottery figures were made in the latter part of the XVIIIth dynasty. Those of Amenemant (U.C. 58, 59), were plain when baked, and engraved afterwards; some black ink shows that they were not stuccoed. Another incised figure of Amenmes (60) has traces of white stucco, and blue colour in the signs. The next step in manufacture was to carve one fine shabti, and then make a mould from it, and thus mould many copies in pottery; such are 61 and 62 of the high priest of Amen, Paser. Plain figures of pottery were used as a base for painting, as in the bust 79 and figure 78. This latter system rapidly degenerated in the XIXth dynasty, from fairly good figures as 123, down to the rudest lumps at 155. Such figures are often inscribed in hieratic, see pl. xiv. For instances of the variety of rough pottery figures found together in the XIXth dynasty, see the groups in *Gizeh and Rifeh* (double volume), pl. xxxvii C.

The next stage was the adoption of glazing for figures. This naturally followed on the great development of glazing under Akhenaten. The shabti was not in favour at the close of the XVIIIth dynasty, but when it revived, glaze became the favourite material. At first glaze was on stone, as the schist figures of Sety I (Florence, U.C. 87, 89) of the vizier Paser (U.C. 93) and a figure of Nekhtamen (Florence). This soon vanished, and glazed pottery alone reigned supreme; beginning under Sety I (as U.C. 90, 91, 92) of fine work, it rapidly degraded. Some of the early examples are striking experiments; an exquisite one is of white glaze inlaid with violet signs (Cairo), some have red glaze faces and hands, and other colours inlaid, as U.C. 222. Under the XXIst dynasty an intense blue was used for the royal figures, but the inscriptions are coarse and very carelessly written. In the XXIInd dynasty the figures degrade to very rough execution, and in the XXIIIrd they become at last almost shapeless and often without any pretence of inscription. In the XXVIth dynasty, glazing was fully revived and was the constant material of shabtis, down to the brilliant ones of Nekht-her-heb.

Mud was used, covered over with a green or blue wash, to imitate glazed figures, in the XXIInd to XXVth dynasties, at last degrading to tiny dumps of plain mud, as U.C. 513. Another treatment of mud was to varnish it over, and inscribe it with yellow paint as U.C. 431, 432.

Exceptional figures are found sometimes, as the solid blue glass shabti with gold leaf bands, found at Abydos, now in Cairo (*El Amrah* xxxix).

41. The number and mode of burial of the shabtis varied much. About the time of Tehutmes III, and on to Ramessu II, single figures were buried on the way to the reputed tomb of Osiris at Abydos. Single figures are likewise found in the tombs from the XIIth dynasty and XVIIIth dynasty; and it seems to be rare to find more than one shabti of a person before the end of the XVIIIth dynasty, except of kings. This accords with the view of the shabti being the substitute for the mummy. The reckoning of the shabtis as servants, which became usual from the rise of the XIXth dynasty, naturally resulted in needing many figures of them, and led to the supply of an overseer. The numbers were yet small about the beginning of the XIXth dynasty; seven in one tomb (*Abydos* III, 50); in another was one of sandstone inscribed, two of limestone and five of rough pottery, uninscribed (*Tanis* II, *Nebesheh*, p. 20). In other tombs 6 glazed, or 2 limestone, or 3 red pottery, 10 glazed and 2 red pot, all of the XIXth dynasty (*Neb.*, p. 32). The royal shabtis of the XXIst dynasty were 75 of Pinezem I, 158 of Ramaka, but the full numbers do not seem to have been published. Of the XXIInd dynasty about 50 are together (p. 33). Of glazed shabtis in the XXVIth dynasty, 11 (1 inscribed), 16 (1 inscribed), 50 (5 inscribed), 325 (3 inscribed), and 266, in different graves (*Neb.*, pp. 21–22). Larger numbers were however quite usual; of the XXVth dynasty at Thebes there were two wooden boxes with each coffin, in one pair 200 and 203, total 403, in another pair 185 and 183, total 368, of rude little figures of mud (*Qurneh* 15). In the XXVIth dynasty at Hawara, the great burial of Horuza had two recesses for shabtis, one containing 203, the other 196, total 399 (*Kahun* 19). These shabtis had been made by many different hands, for 17 varieties of style could be traced; as the number of each style was always irregular, and different from the others, it seems that the making was not sub-let to workmen, but was done in one large factory. As late as the XXXth dynasty, at Abydos, a burial in the tomb of Zeher had two boxes, with 198 and 196 figures, total 394. The burial of Pedu-asar son of Zeher had 385 figures (*Abydos* I, 38, 39). A later burial (undated) at Abusir el Melek contained 365 ushabtis (*Z.A.S.* 1904, 8). In Cairo is a group of 397 figures of Pehem (LORET 507–904).

One view has been proposed that the Abusir find was to provide a figure for each day of the year; and a shabti (Berlin) with a month and day marked on it, has been considered to support this view (*Z.A.S.* 1904, 8). Unless we had several different days named on one group, the day might as likely be the day of death, or even the day of birth for a horoscope. That the numbers are in no other case 365 contradicts the year-day idea. Then it has been proposed that there were 365 and 1 overseer for every 10 men, or 401 in all. The actual totals stated above are 368, 403, 399, 394, 385, 397; none of them agreeing with either number proposed. The main objection to the addition of a tenth of overseers is that there were no figures of overseers in these six groups of about 400: the figures were all alike in form, and we can only suppose that the purpose was to deposit about 400.

In the XVIIIth dynasty the sole shabti was sometimes placed in a model coffin of wood or pottery. In the XIXth dynasty, round pots were often made for this purpose, which have been confounded with canopic jars as they had heads of the four sons of Horus upon them; yet their contents were from 6 to 12 ushabtis of pottery (*El Amrah*, p. 78, lvi). Square boxes of pottery were also used for the rough pottery shabtis, pl. xxxiv. Later, wooden boxes of the form of a round-topped shrine were usual (*Qurneh* liii) sometimes painted on the sides with figures of the gods.

There is one curious evidence that the inscriptions were in some instances recited to the makers, who wrote down what they heard. There is at Bologna a shabti inscribed for Psemthek, son of Thes-net-peru, and one at Florence for the son of Thes-net-meru. Such an error could never arise in reading by eye, but would easily be due to mistaken hearing.

We have now reviewed the gradual changes and growth of an intimate subject of Egyptian thought, and seen how it was influenced by the revolutions of the civilisation. The beautiful work of the XIIth dynasty became degraded to rough sticks in the XVIIth; the noble figures of the XVIIIth rapidly waned to the rough granite and coarse wood, supplanted by a revival in fine glaze which degraded into mud dumps in the XXIIIrd; finally, the Ethiopian revival of the art in fine stone, dwindled in the XXXth dynasty to the roughest pottery. The Greek domination ended the ushabti, as also the scarab; the inherent ideas of Egypt were outworn, and the civilisation could never retrace its steps as it had repeatedly done before.

CHAPTER VII

TRANSLITERATION OF NAMES OF USHABTIS AT UNIVERSITY COLLEGE.

(Materials uninscribed. 1 Wood. 2 Pottery. 3 Black Serpentine. 3a, White Limestone. 4 Wood. 5 and onward, see reference in catalogue by names.)

5–7 Teta. 8, 9 Teta-an. 10–17 Teta-sa-antef. 18–23 Teta-nefer. 24–7 Teta-on. 28 Antef. 29, 29A Tehuti. 30 Ta-nehesyt. 31 User. 32 Antef. 33–4 Hetep-sa.

35 Tha. 36 Tunefer. 42–3 Sen-hetep. 44 Sa-ra. 45 Sa-pa-art. 46 Aohmes-sa-paar.

XVIIIth dynasty. 47 Sen-em-aoh. 48 Nehi. 49. Monuna. 50 Baka. 51 Aniy. 52 User-hot. 53 Ra-em-heb. 55 Mes. 56 Pe-kharu. 58–9 Amenemant. 60 Amen-mes. 61–2 Pa-ser. 63 Huy. 65 Amen-hetep (II). 66 Minmes. 67 Hather-pert. 68 Sadiomia. 69 Hentmehy. 70 Urt-neb-nefert. 71 Mer-ant. 73 Thay. 74 Set . . . 75 Mohu. 76 User-hot-amen-em-neheh. 77 Mehy-hetep. 78 Neteth-khenti. 79 Kana. 80 Amen-hetep (III). 81–2 Akhenaten. 83 Kanure.

XIXth dynasty. 85 User-menth. 86–92 Sety (I). 93–5 Pa-ser. 96 Ta-ast. 99 Kho-em-uas (son of Ramessu II). 100 Huy. 102 Thenure. 103 Nashu. 104 Ramessu. 105 Set-mes. 106 Mehy-hetep. 107 Hetep-asa. 108 Khnem-em-ua. 109 Piam. 110 Hent-nefu. 112–3 Bu-ar-er-tu-khemt. 114 Sunure. 115 Auy. 118–9 Hent-ur. 120 Baka. 121 Ymuda-taurt. 122 Nefer-ob-heb. 123 Res-su. 124 Mes. 125 Nekhtru-amen. 126 Kanure. 127 Khnem-pa-taui. 128 Shed-mes. 129 Mut-em-per. 130 Nafi. 131 Sebek-mes. 132 User-menth. 133 Nefer-her. 134 Kho-em . . . 135 Moaa. 136 Hot-aay. 137 Nefer-her. 138 Au. 139 Pa-ra-khou. 140 Thay-mes. 141 Bakuu, Nenoy. 142 Ast. 147–8 female figures with overseer. 152 Her-kho. Next a canopic pot of Hapi brother of Her, for priestess of lord of Matenu (Atfih), Rest. 153 Pay-denurga. 156 Rames. 157–8 Nerau-nefer. 159 Nes-pe-uah-maot. 160 Sunure. 162 User-menthu. 163 Amen-em-apt. 164 Ta-user. 165 Mery-ra. 166 Aymy. 167 Nefer-hetep. 168–9 Huy. 170–1 Nes-mut. 172–3 Nef-per-pa. 174–5 Mery-mo. 176 Hent-ef-nefer. 177 Neheh-neferta. 178 Ta-ur-em-her. 181 Ramessu-er-neheh. 182 Pa-ra-em-nenu-ra-neb. 183–4 Nefer-renpet. 185 Res-su. 190 Nefer-am. 191 Bak-amen. 192 Patnub-heb. 195 User-maot-ra-nekhtu. 196 Payutu-heri. 197 Meru-onkh. 198 Ta-ua-shed. 199 Amen-mes. 200 Mutnefert. 201 Bak-amen. 202 Hetep-mut. 203 Ta-urt. 204 Ta-on. 205 Ta-nekhtu-ra. 206 On-mut. 207 Oat-urt . . . 210 Nefu-nefer. 211 Pazay. 212 Neferu. 214 Mentu-hetep. 215 . . . Hat-her. 216 Suah, Sahu? 217 Mer-f . . . 219 Ta-nes. 220 Nebtu-her-ta. 221 Sebek-hetep.

Glazed pottery. XIXth dynasty. 222 Aaă. 223 Pa-ser. 224 Ast. 225 Refuy. 226 Urta. 227 Nekht-amen. 232 Nezem. 233 Ra-user-maot-nekht. 234 Nes-pa-ra. 235 Nefer-ta. 236 Amen-hetep. 237 Tehuti-mes. 238 Amen-mes. 239 Ray-ra. 240 Tehuti-mes. 241–2 Nes-pa-ra. 244–5 Amen-em-ant.

XXth dynasty. 247 Ramessu (IV). 248 Ramessu (VI). 250 Nehay. 253 Her.

XXIst dynasty, blue glaze. 254 Hent-taui (queen of Pionkh). 255 Painezem. 256 Kheper-kho-ra, setep-ne-amen (Painezem I). 257 Kheper-kho-ra. 258 Maot-ka-ra (queen of Painezem I). 260 Men-kheper-ra. 261 Mysa-hert. 262 Ast-ne-khebt (queen of Men-kheper-ra). 263 Hent-taui (queen of Nesi-ba-neb-zedu). 264 Pa-nezem (II). 265 Nesi-khensu (queen of Panezem II).

XXIst–XXIInd dynasties. 267 Mut-em-hot (queen of Usarken II). 268–9 Mut-mery, meht-ne-usekht (queen of Usarken II). 270 Menth-em-heb. 271 Res-thu. 272 Yimadua. 273 Pedu-amen. 274 Pipay. 275 Nesi-amen. 276 Nes-pa-her-on. 277 Amen-hetep. 278 Amen-hot-pa-masha (?). 279 Her. 280 Usarken. 281 Sekhmetu (?). 282 Pa-kharua. 283 Zed-ptah (auf-onkh), (son of Takerat II). 284 Pa-kharu. 287 Nef-nezem. 288 Mery. 289–90 Huy. 291 Hotu (?). 292 Nes-pa-ka (shuti). 293 Nes-neb-taui. 294 Bak-ne-mut. 295–7 Merth-ne-amen. 298 Nesi-aohta, see 312. 299 Pedu-mut. 300 Pa-pes-sa. 301 Her-ub . . . 302 Nes-ta-uzat-aakhet. 303 Thay-nefer. 304 Em-kak-ra. 305 Ast-em-kheb. 306 Thent-mau. 307 Hent-taui. 308 Pa-shed-ne-khensu. 309–10 Nes-pa-her-ne-hot. 311 Then-amen. 312 Nesi-aohta, see 298. 313 Thet-du-amen. 314 Zed-menth-auf-onkh. 315 Zed-her-onkh. 316 Nesi-mut. 317 Neb-zed-ast. 318 Thent-her-kena. 319 Ta-nekht-mut. 320 Zed (or Nes-)ne-amen. 321 Nesi-hetep-amen. 322 Nesi-amen. 323 Nes-menth. 324 Tehuti-mes. 325 Pa-nes-taui (?). 326 Hent-taui. 329 Zedi-hetep-mut. 330 Ast. 331 Ast. 332 Yi-hetep-em-mut. 333–4 Nes-pa-nub. 335 Nebt-neheh. 336 Neb-neheht. 337–8 Her-taui. 339 Her-sekhen-ast. 340 Her-khebt. 341 Her. 342 Zetta-set (?). 343 Shaq-sha or Ha-qe-ha. 344 Bak-khensu. 345 Ym-hetep. 346 Zed-mut. 347 Pa-shed-khensu. 348 Thent-shedot. 349 Thent-th-shedu. 351 Pa-shed-khensu. 352–3 User-hot. 354 Menth-aus-onkh. 355 Ta-nebu-net. 356 Buararuhot. 357 Ta-nebu-net. 358 Mena Duat. 359 Pa-khred-ne-ast. 360 Men-am. 361–2 Bakhet. 363 Baky. 365 Neb-her-thes (?). 366 Thent-du-amen. 367 Ra-mes-user-taui. 368 Oa-za-dep. 369 Net-urt. 370 Bak-khensu. 371 Amen (?). 372 Padu-amen. 373 Nesy-neb-taui. 374 Her. 375 Her-mut-nekht-khensu. 376–7 Pa-nekht-es-maot. 378 Padu-pa . . . 379 Buareru, see 356. 380 Tehuti. 382 Pa-du-amen. 383 Khensu-mes. 384 Thent-nun. 385 Onkh-ef-ne-khensu. 386 Her.

Green painted clay. 390–1 Onkh. 392 Onkhef. 393 Bak-ne-khensu. 394 Bak-ra. 395–6 Nes-ta-nezem. 397 Onkh-es-ne-mut. 399 Onkh-ef-amen. 400 Onkh-ef-ne-khensu. 401 Neb-aakhety. 402 Neb-aakhet-per.

403 Neb-aakhety. 404 Pa-user-amen. 405 Nesi-hetep-amen. 406 Onkh-es-ast. 407 Bak-ne-mut.

Coarse green glaze, faded. 408 Nes-pa-hent-taui. 409 Nes-pa-her. 410 Hot. 411 Teduament.

Wood painted black. 424 Pa-ari. 425 Bak-ne-khensu. 426 Hent-ma-amten (?). 427–8 Ur. 429 Huy. 430 Dada-sebek-mes. 431–2 Zed-khensu-auf-onkh.

Pottery painted. 433 Nes-ptah. 434–5 Onkhu-mut. 436–7 Hot . . . 438 Ast. 439 Amen-her . . . 442 Pa-dut-khensu. 443 Nes-mut. 444 Zedu-maot-ast-onkh. 445 Pedu-her. 446 Khenm-khert-ne-khensu. 447 Pa-duat-ament. 448 Arer . . . 449 Onkhef-khensu. 450 Ta-bak-khensu. 451 Pa-du-amen. 453 Khenm-khert-ne-khensu. 454 Kha-os. 456 Nes-amen. 457 Nekhtu. 458 Pa-kharu. 459 Then-amen. 460 Onkhef-ne-khensu. 461 Onkhes-pa . . .

Green glaze. XXIInd dynasty. 464–5 Uasarken, High Priest of Memphis. 466 Pedu-mut. 468 Hera. 469–72 Pa-tehuti. 473 Onkhes-en-ast. 474 Amenardas. 475–6 Uasarken, High Priest of Hermopolis. 477–8 Zed-bast-auf-onkh. 478 Great God (King) over the enemy Dut-pa . . . 479–80 Pa-duat. 481 Nes-khensu. 484 King Ra-user-maot, setep-ne-amen, sa-ra-amen-mer, sa-ne-Bastet (Sheshenq III). 485–8 Thes-theren. 493–4 Zed-tehuti-es-onkh. 495 Nes-mut-onkhet. 518 Nes-mut-seonkh. 531 Ast-ne-kheb (dau. Shabaka).

Incised stone. XXVth dynasty. 532–4 Pedu-amen-apt, standard text. 535–8 Amen-ardas (queen). 539 King's dau. of Paonkhy, queen Shep-en-apt. 540 Harua (Assasif tomb). 542 Anher-mes. 543 Prince Nesptah born of Shebnet-sopdu.

Incised glaze. XXVIth dynasty. 544 Tehuti-her. 545 Nes-her. 546 Pa-nef-anet. 547–53 Her-uza. 554 Aohmes-nefer-sekhmet. 554 and 557 older figures, reused with altered name. 555 Psemthek. 556 Pamau High priest, Thebes. 557 Asar-ardus. 558 Psemthek-ptah-mer. 560 Her-em-hetep. 561 Her-taui. 562 King Aohmes-sanet. 563 Her. 564 Zeher. 565–6 Zeser. 567 Hapnen. 568 Dut-em-hetepy-net. 569 Her-uza. 570 King Ra-uah-ab (Apries). 571 Ra-uah-ab-neb-heb. 572 Hesu. 573 Queen Net-khadeb-ar-bent (mother of Nekht-neb-ef). 574–6, 9 King Nekht-her-heb. 577 Tha-ne-heb. 578 Psem-thek.

Band and column inscribed. 580 Uah-ab-ra-em-aakhet. 582 Psemthek-onkh. 583 Her. 584 Oha. 585 Her. 586 Hap-men. 587 Aohmes. 589 Aohmes. 590 born of Renpet-nefer. 591 Uah-ab-ra. 592 Ka-em-hesuia. 593 An-hetepu. 594–7 Thent-aqera. 595 Ast-dus. 598 Amen-ardas. 599 Nayroarud. 601 Tehuti-em-hot. 602 Aohmes. 603, 8 Uza-her-ne-nesut-per. 607 Uah-ab-ra-ptah-mer. 609 Pa-du-amen. 610, 11, see 554. 612, 14 Ymhetep. 613 Pe-sa-ahet. 615 Pe-du-bastet. 616 Mera. 617 Arer.

Narrow, usually inscribed back pillar. XXVII–XXXth dynasty. 620 Her-kheb. 621 Auf-oa. 622 Un-men-hap. 623 Her. 624 Atmu-hetep. 625 Hepa. 626 Ptah-hetep. 628 Aoh-mes. 632 Apentet-neb-em. 634 Pe-du-ptah. 635–8 Hen-ka. 639 Mentu-hetep.

Latest class. 641 Zeher. 642 Pe-hoti. 643–4, 9 Pe-du-asar. 645 Neferu. 646–8 Zeher. 651–5 uninscribed in tomb of Zeher (*Abydos* I, 37–9).

INDEX

FORMULA TO MID XVIIITH DYNASTY.

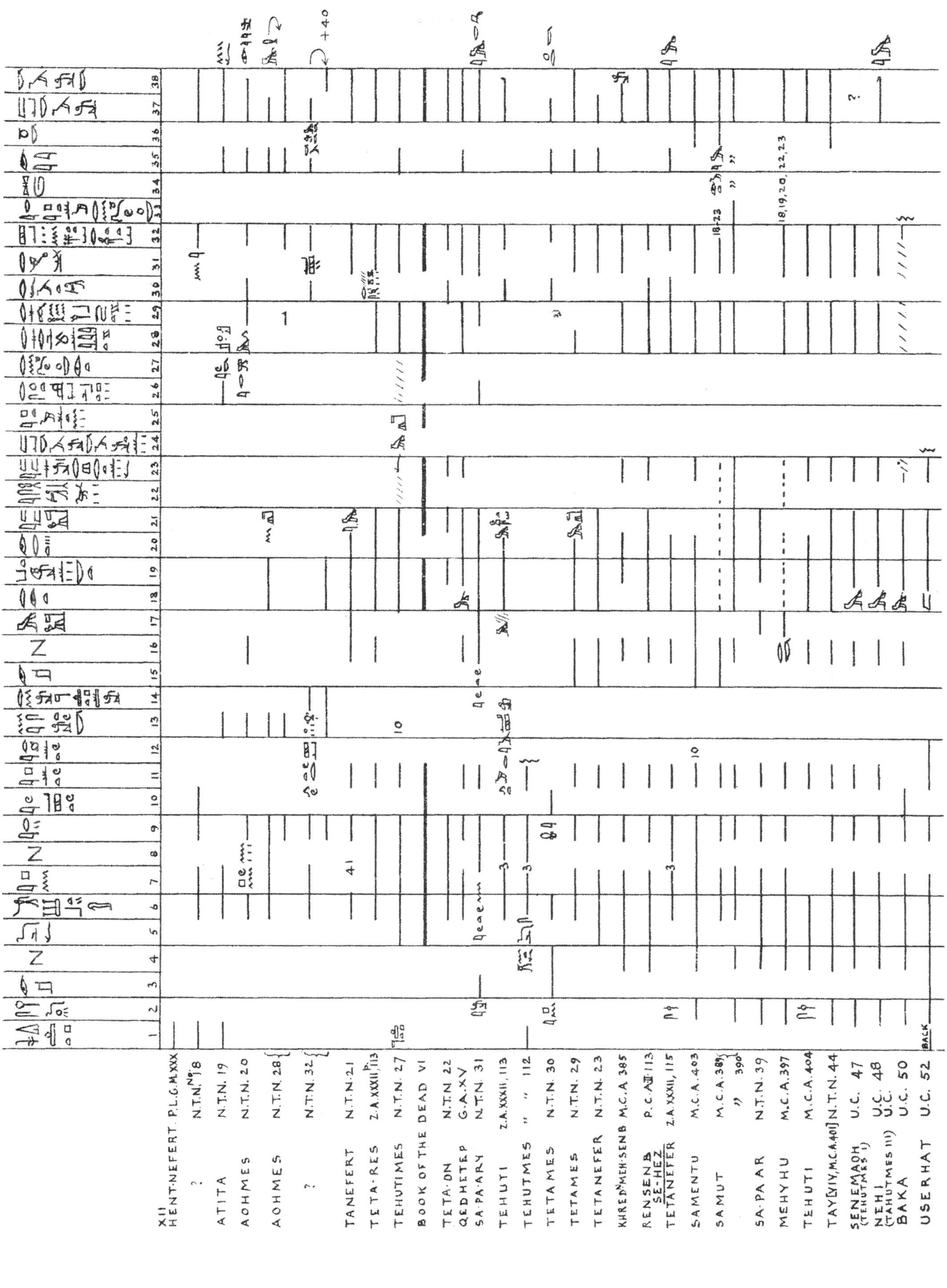

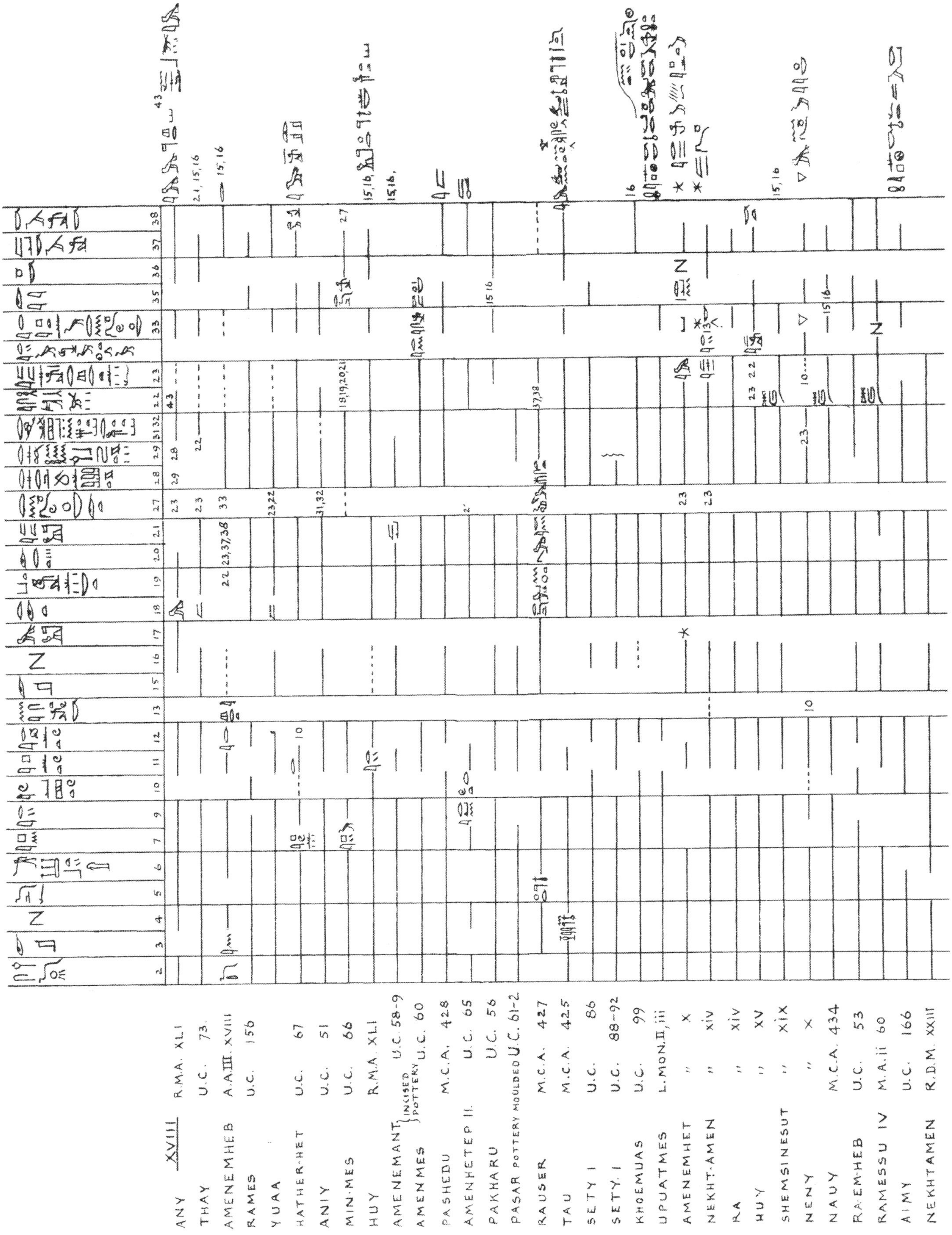
2 3 4 5 6 7 9 10 11 12 13 15 16 17 18 19 20 21 27 28 29 31 32 22 23 33 35 36 37 38
XVIII
ANY R.M.A. XLI
THAY U.C. 73.
AMENEMHEB A.A.III. XVIII
RAMES U.C. 156
YUAA
HATHER-HET U.C. 67
ANIY U.C. 51
MIN-MES U.C. 66
HUY R.M.A. XLI
AMENEMANT INCISED POTTERY U.C. 58-9
AMENMES U.C. 60
PASHEDU M.C.A. 428
AMENHETEP II. U.C. 65
PAKHARU U.C. 56
PASAR POTTERY MOULDED U.C. 61-2
RAUSER M.C.A. 427
TAU M.C.A. 425
SETY I U.C. 86
SETY I U.C. 88-92
KHOEMUAS U.C. 99
UPUATMES L. MON. II, iii
AMENEMHET " x
NEKHT-AMEN " xiv
RA " xiv
HUY " xv
SHEMSINESUT " xix
NENY " x
NAUY M.C.A. 434
RA-EM-HEB U.C. 53
RAMESSU IV M.A. ii 60
AIMY U.C. 166
NEKHTAMEN R.D.M. XXIII

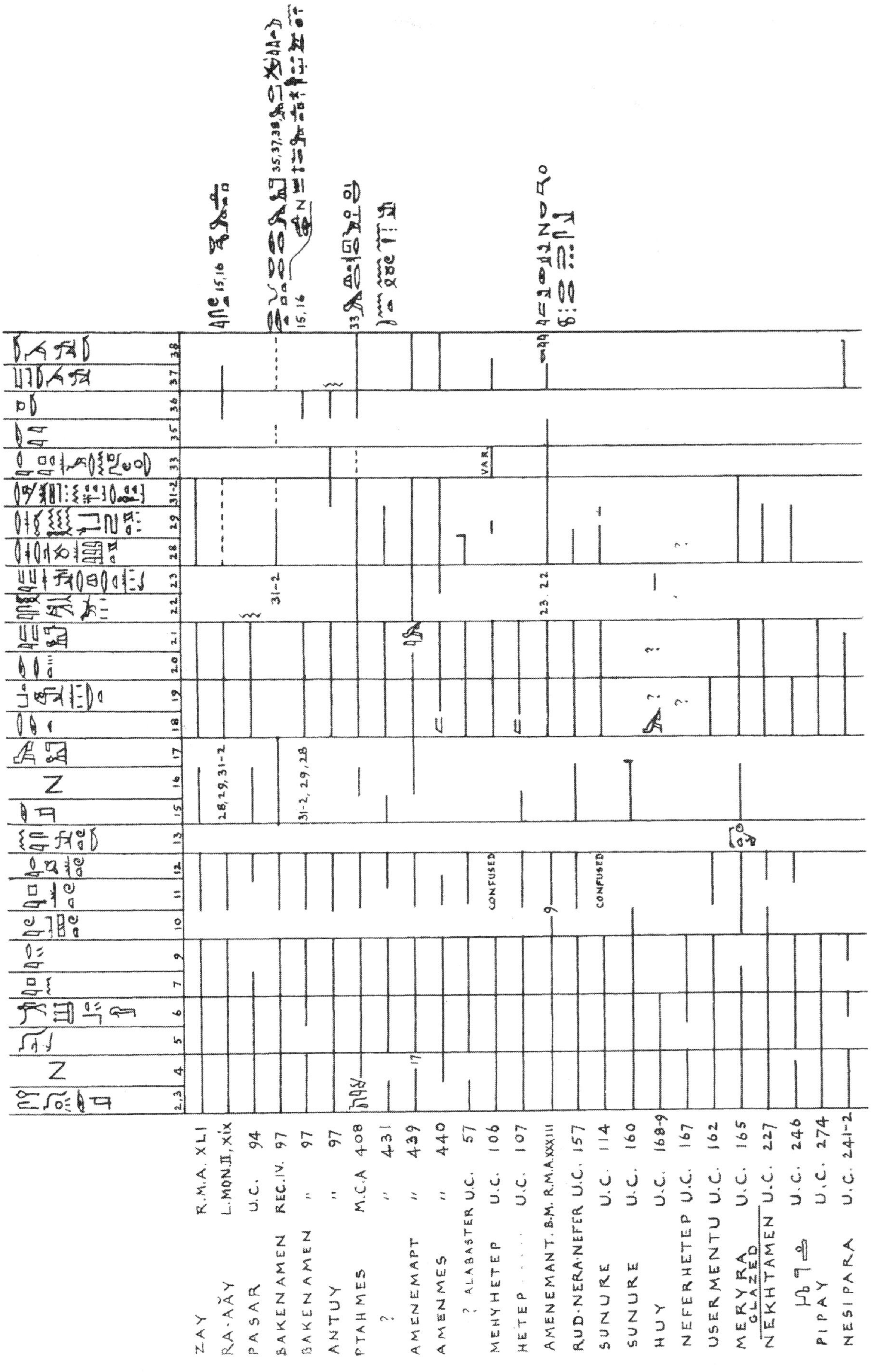
2,3
4
5
6
7
9
10
11
12
13
15
16
17
18
19
20
21
22
23
28
29
31-2
33
35
36
37
38
ZAY R.M.A. XLI
RA-AĂY L.MON.II, xix
PASAR U.C. 94
BAKENAMEN REC.IV. 97
BAKENAMEN " 97
ANTUY " 97
PTAHMES M.C.A 408
? " 431
AMENEMAPT " 439
AMENMES " 440
? ALABASTER U.C. 57
MENYHETEP U.C. 106
HETEP .... U.C. 107
AMENEMANT. B.M. R.M.A.XXIII
RUD-NERA-NEFER U.C. 157
SUNURE U.C. 114
SUNURE U.C. 160
HUY U.C. 168-9
NEFERHETEP U.C. 167
USERMENTU U.C. 162
MERYRA GLAZED U.C. 165
NEKHTAMEN U.C. 227
U.C. 246
PIPAY U.C. 274
NESIPARA U.C. 241-2
28, 29, 31-2
31-2, 29, 28
31-2
23. 22
CONFUSED
CONFUSED
VAR.
15, 16
35, 37, 38
33

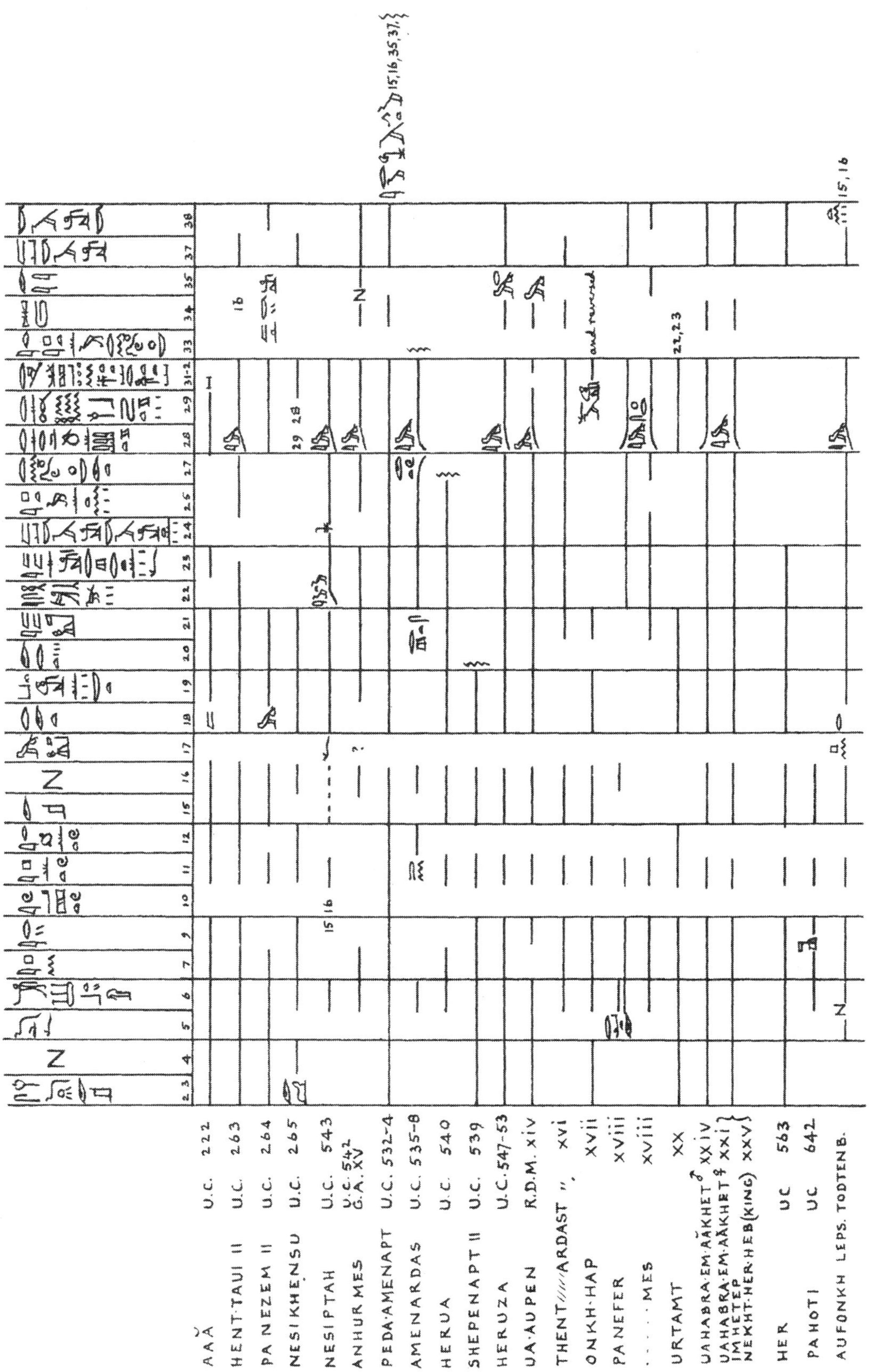
AAĂ U.C. 222
HENT·TAUI II U.C. 263
PANEZEM II U.C. 264
NESIKHENSU U.C. 265
NESIPTAH U.C. 543
ANHURMES U.C. 542 G.A. XV
PEDA·AMENAPT U.C. 532-4
AMENARDAS U.C. 535-8
HERUA U.C. 540
SHEPENAPT II U.C. 539
HERUZA U.C. 547-53
UA·AUPEN R.D.M. xiv
THENT////ARDAST " xvi
ONKH·HAP xvii
PANEFER xviii
....MES xviii
URTAMT xx
UAHABRA·EM·AAKHET ♂ xxiv
UAHABRA·EM·AAKHET ♀ xxi
IMHETEP NEKHT·HER·HEB (KING) xxv
HER UC 563
PAHOTI UC 642
AUFONKH LEPS. TODTENB.
2.3 4 5 6 7 9 10 11 12 15 16 17 18 19 20 21 22 23 24 26 27 28 29 31-2 33 34 35 37 38
15,16,35,37
15,16
and reversed
22,23

1. if one summons thee

2. „ „ Tetares if one numbers
3. O „ „ „ „ „
4. Osiris Tetamesu „ „ „ „ „
5. Make clear Nehi says he „ „ „ „ „
6. „ „ „ Userhot „ „ „ „ „ „ „ 6. if one reckons
7. „ „ Any „ „ „ „ „ „ „ „ „ „
8. „ „ „ Peduamenapt „ „ „ „ „ „ „ „ „ „

2. Tetares
3. Qedhetep
4. Tetamesu
5. Nehi
7. Any in
8. Osiris Peduamenapt

Make clear Osiris N says he O Shuabti this, N, if one calls, if one numbers, if one reckons, if one summons thee N

1. to do all works of Kherneter
2. „ „ „ that are to be done in „
3. in „ „ „ „ „ „ „
4. to do „ „ „ „ „ „ „
5. in „ „ „ „ „ there „ „
6. „ „ „ „ „ „ „ „
7. „ „ „ „ „ „ „
8. „ „ „ „ „ „ „ „ „

7. then shalt thou smite for him evils
8. „ „ „ „ „ there

3. as a man at his affairs
5. „ „ „
6. „ „ „
7. „ „ „
8. „ „ „

to do all works that are to be done, there in Kherneter, then shalt thou smite for him evils there, as a man at his affairs.

1. to cause to be full the channels
2. to cause to grow the fields, „ „ „
3. „ „ „ „ „ „
4. „ „ „ „ „ „
5. „ „ „ „ „ „
6. „ „ „ „ „ „
7. „ „ „ „ „ „
„ „ „ „ „ „

8. Behold him say thou, if one numbers, at any time

Behold him say thou, if one numbers, at any time to act there to cause to grow the fields, to cause to be full the channels.

1. or sand east for west
2. to transport the sand of the „ to the „
3. „ „ „ „
4. „ „ west east
5. „ „ east west
6. „ „
7. „ „ „ „
8. „ „ *west* *east* and *vice versa*

7. if numbered at any time

1. I am doing, reply thou as a servant if summoned
2. Behold me say thou
3. „ „ „ „
4. „ „ „ „
5. „ „
Me „ „ in
8. „ „

to transport the sand of the east to the west and *vice versa* if numbered at any time I am doing Me Behold me say thou

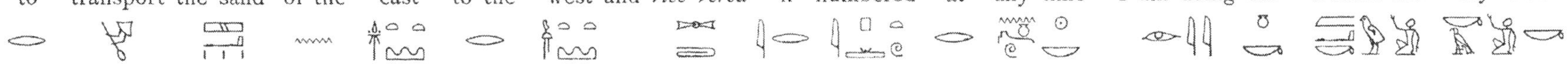

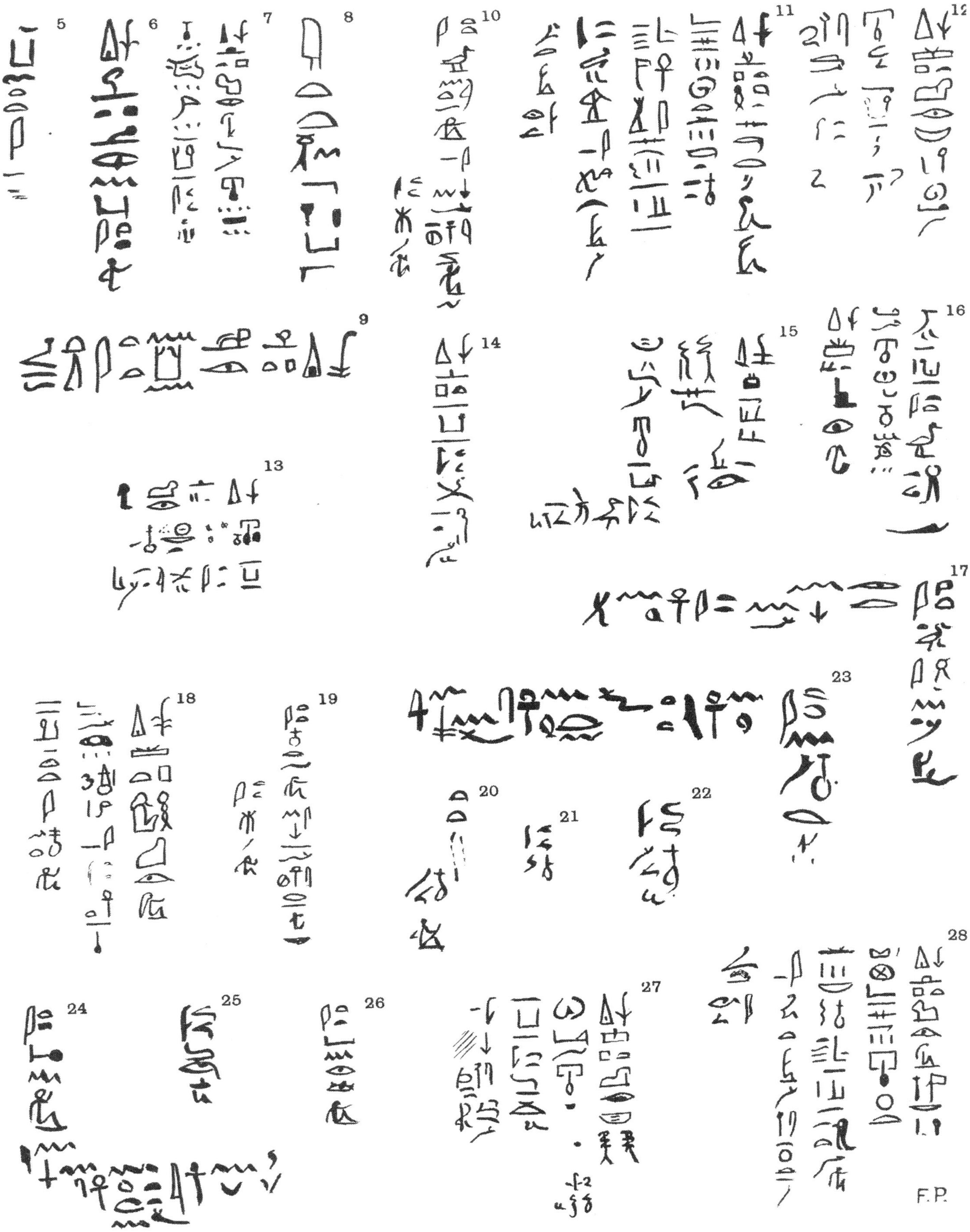
5
6
7
8
10
11
12
9
14
15
16
13
17
18
19
23
20
21
22
28
27
24
25
26
F.P.

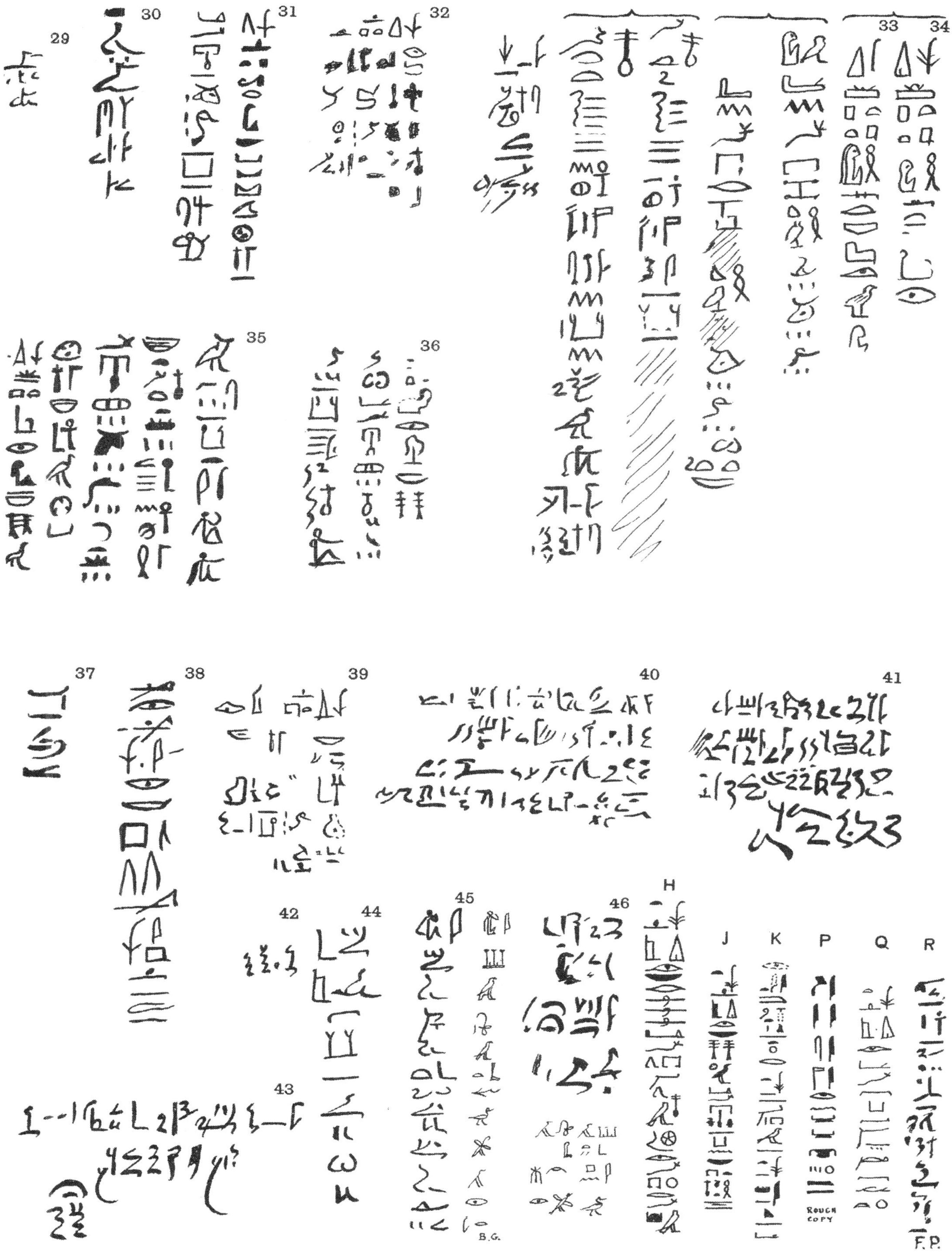

29
30
31
32
33
34
35
36
37
38
39
40
41
42
43
44
45
46
H
J
K
P
Q
R
ROUGH COPY
B.G.
F.P.

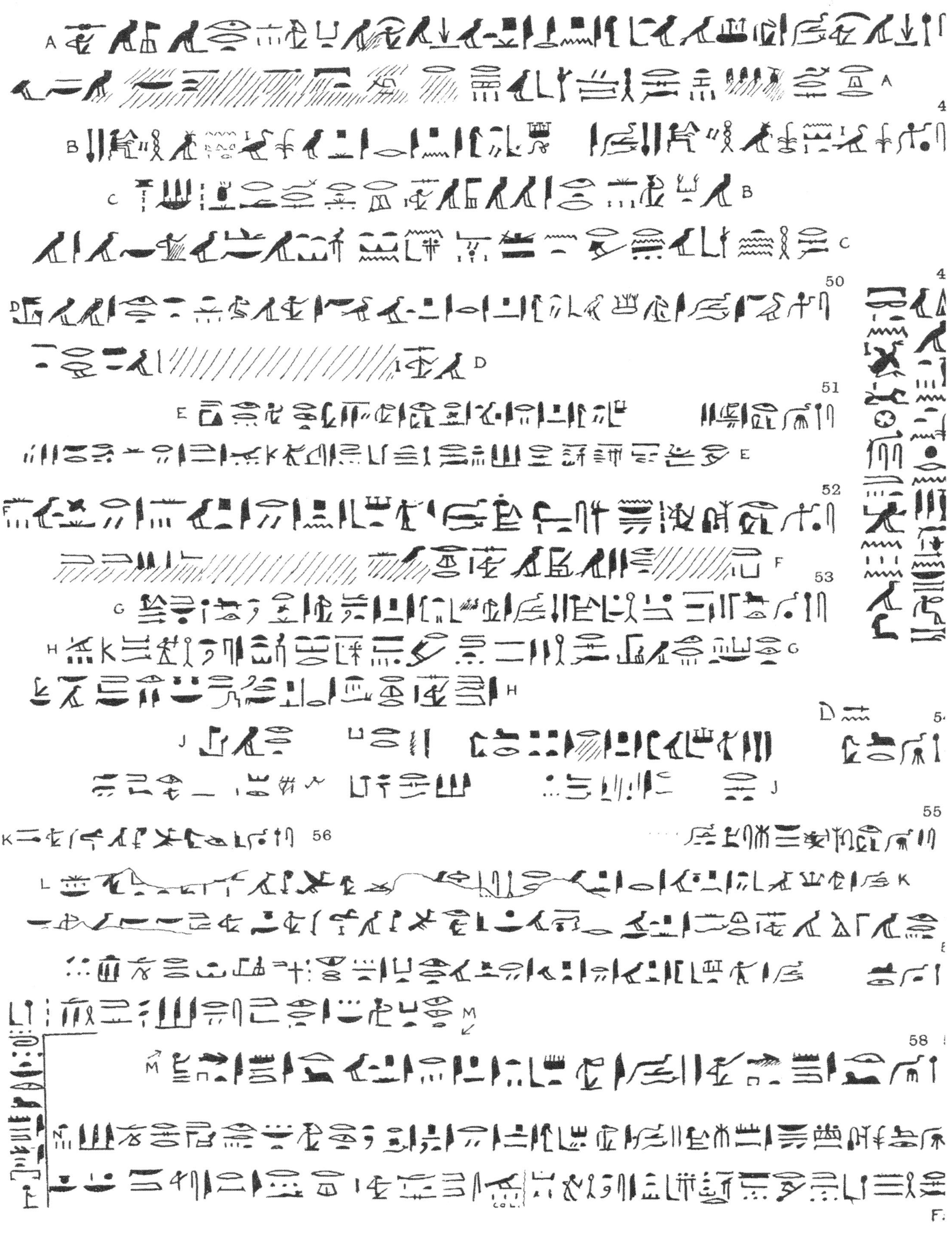
A
A
B
C
B
C
50
D
D
51
E
E
52
F
F
53
G
H
G
H
D
J
J
55
K
56
L
K
M
M
58
N
COL.
F

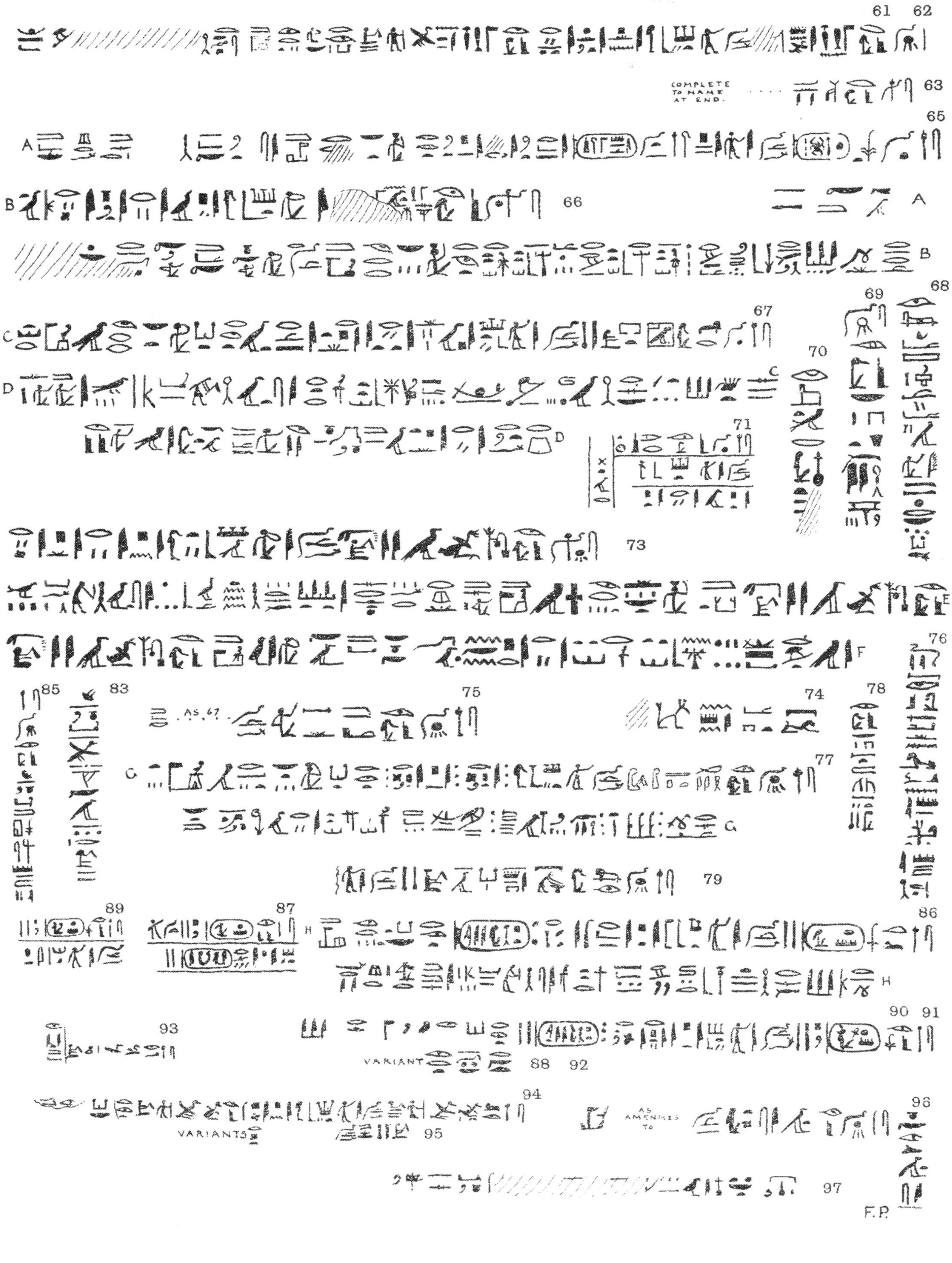
61 62
COMPLETE TO NAME AT END.
63
65
A
B
66
67
68
69
70
C
D
71
73
E
F
76
85
83
75
74
78
AS. 67
G
77
79
89
87
H
86
93
90 91
VARIANT
88 92
94
VARIANTS
95
AS AMENMES TO
96
97
F.P.

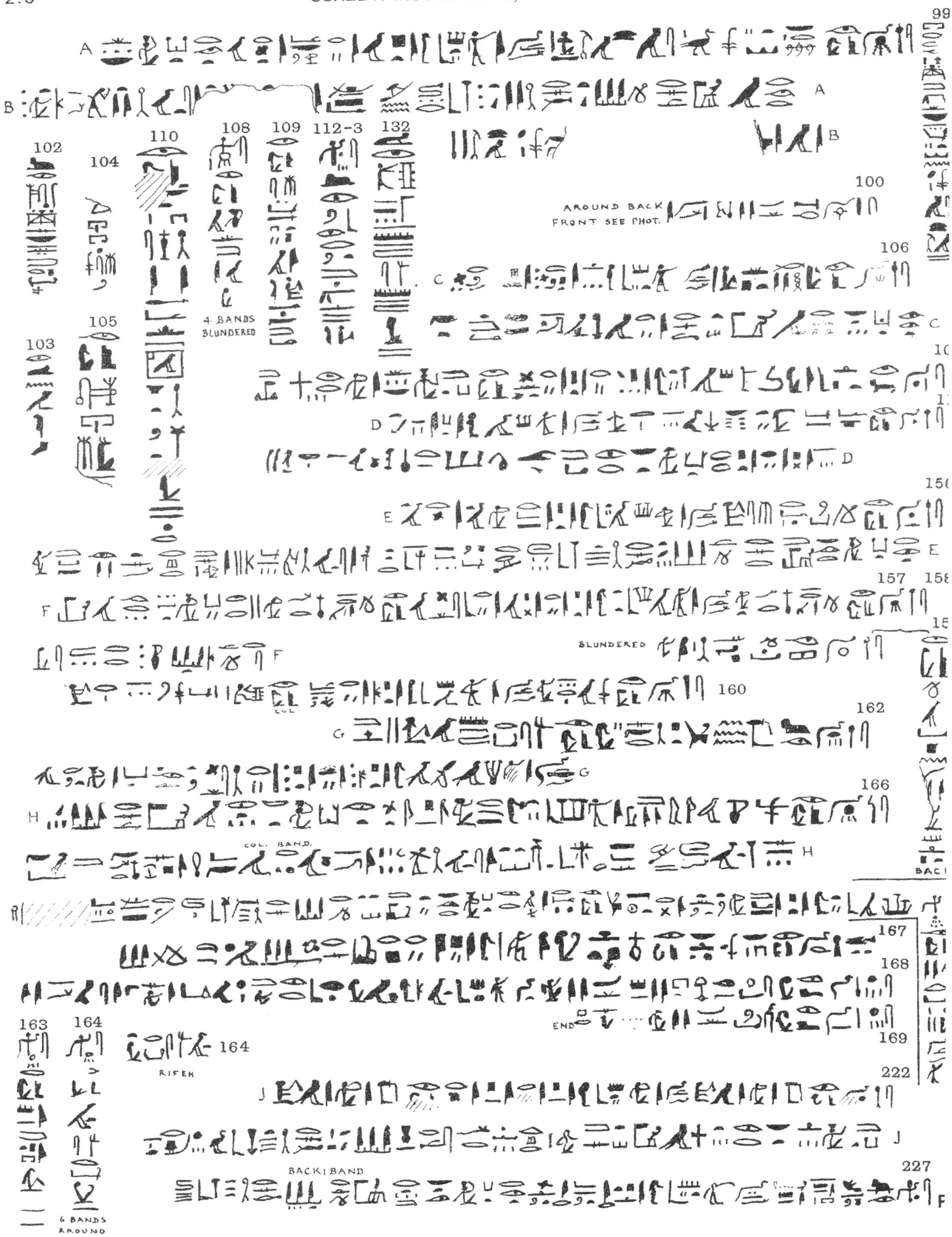
99
A
B
102
104
105
103
110
108
4 BANDS BLUNDERED
109
112-3
132
100
AROUND BACK FRONT SEE PHOT.
106
C
D
E
156
157
158
F
BLUNDERED
160
COL.
162
G
166
H
COL. BAND.
167
168
169
END
163
164
RIFEH
6 BANDS AROUND
222
J
BACK BAND
227

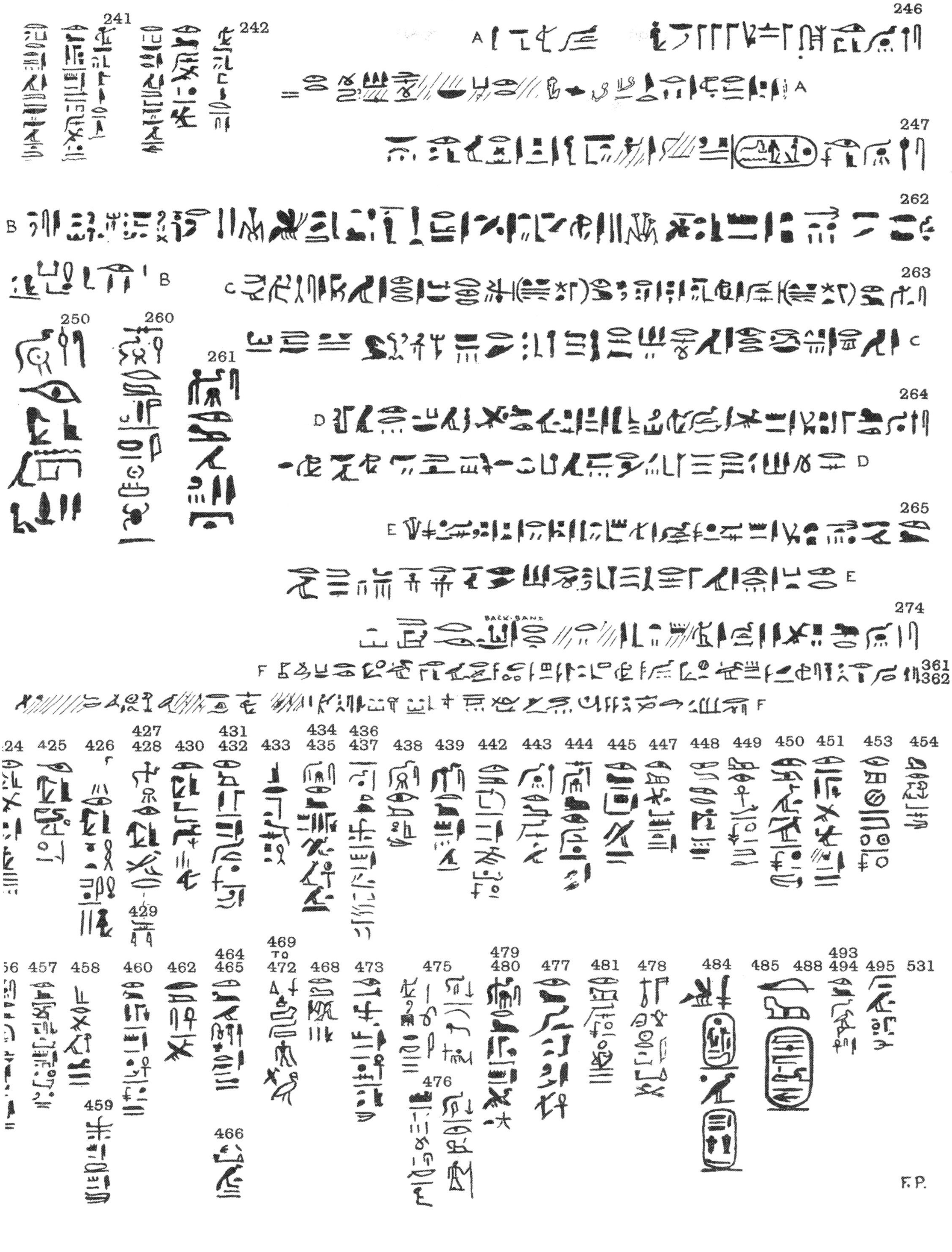
241
242
246
A
A
247
262
B
B
C
263
250
260
261
C
264
D
D
265
E
E
274
BACK-BAND
F
361
362
F
24 425 426 427 428 429 430 431 432 433 434 435 436 437 438 439 442 443 444 445 447 448 449 450 451 453 454
56 457 458 459 460 462 464 465 466 469 TO 472 468 473 475 476 479 480 477 481 478 484 485 488 493 494 495 531

F.P.

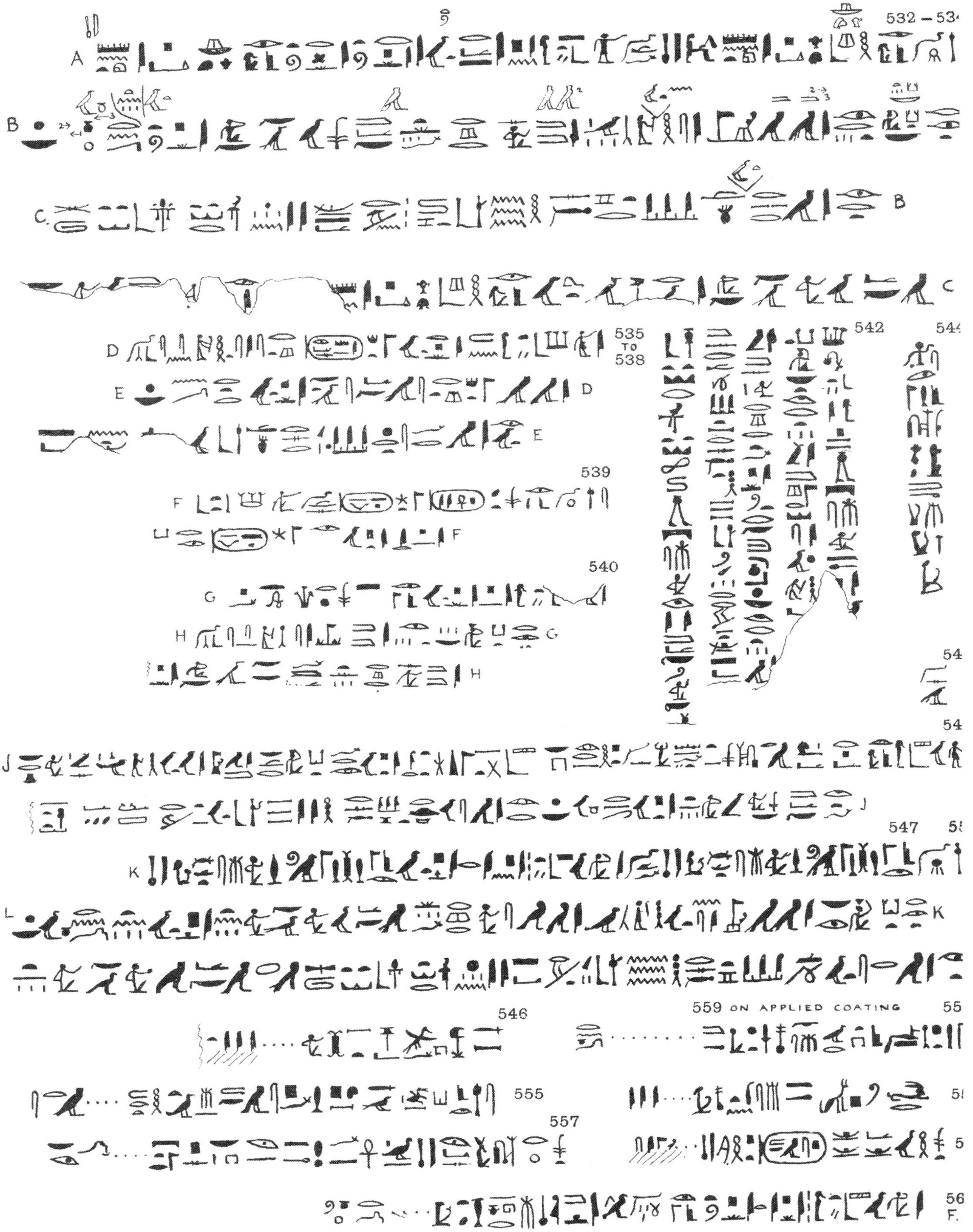
535 TO 538
539
540
542
547
546
559 ON APPLIED COATING
555
557

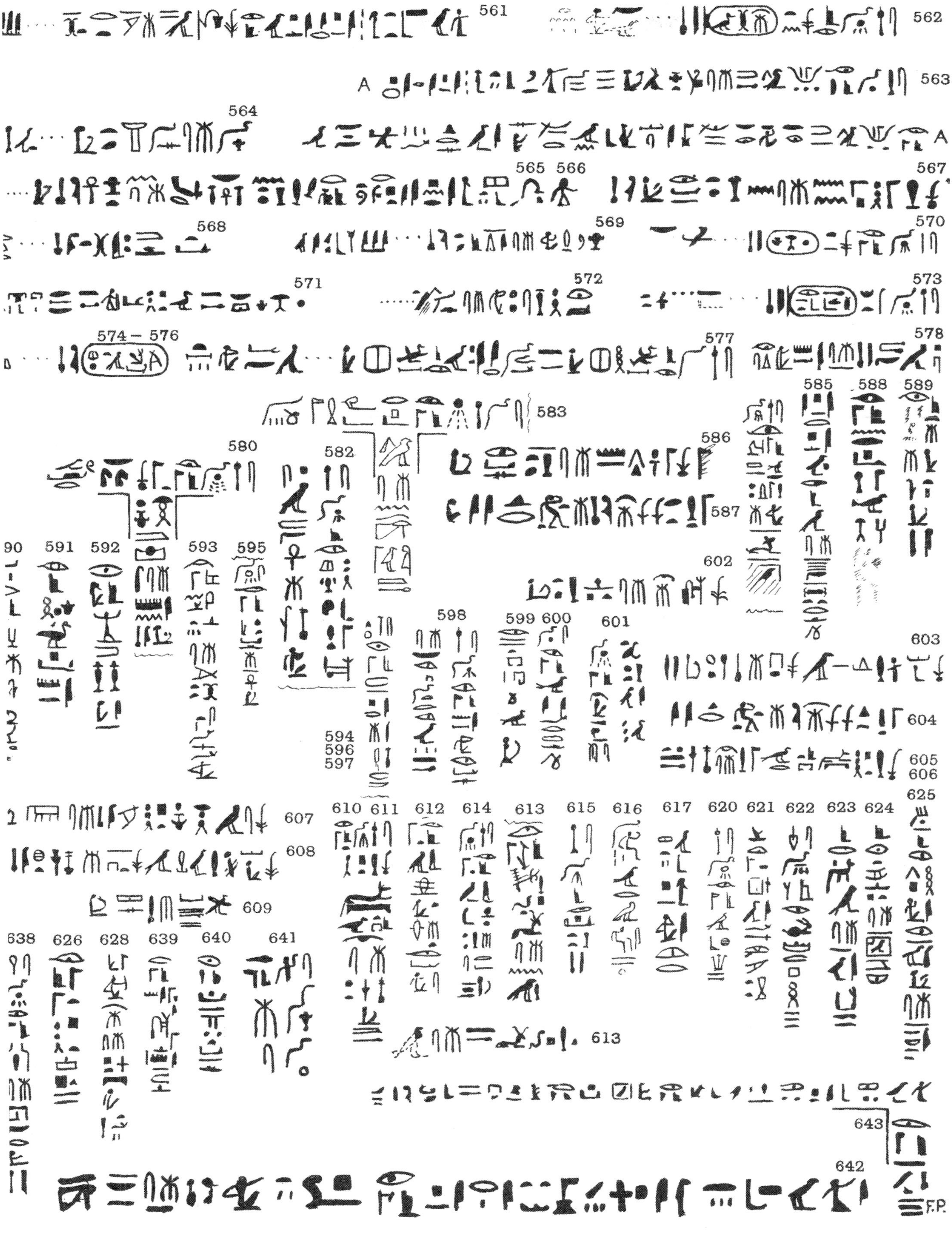
561
562
563
564
565 566
567
568
569
570
571
572
573
574 – 576
577
578
580
582
583
585
586
587
588
589
590
591
592
593
595
598
599 600
601
602
603
604
594
596
597
605
606
625
607
608
609
610 611
612
614
613
615
616
617
620
621
622
623
624
638
626
628
639
640
641
613
643
642
F.P.

122
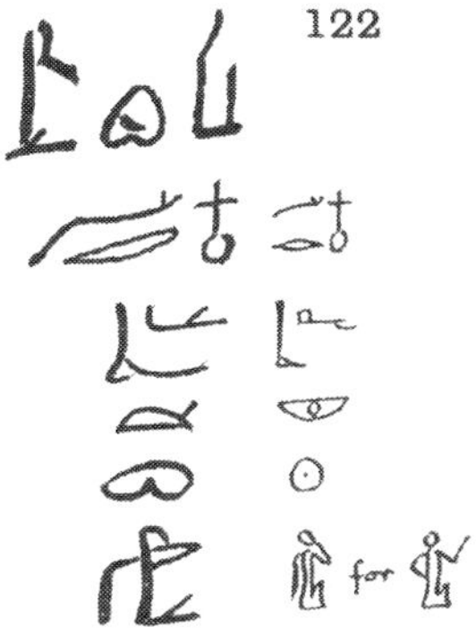

138

139
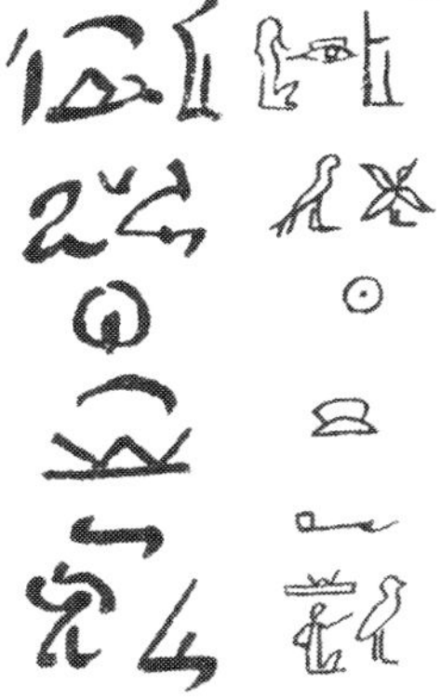

14
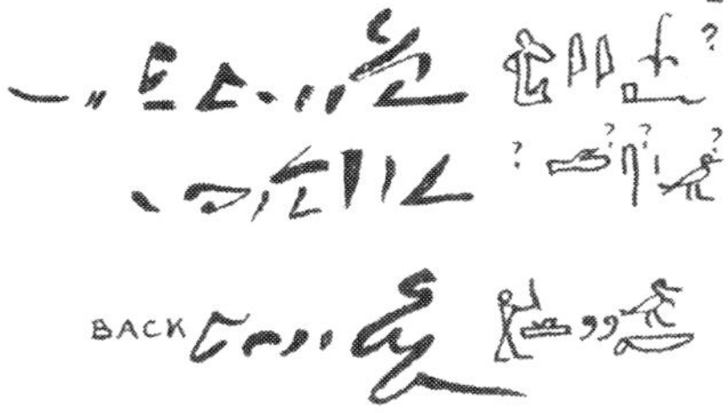

220
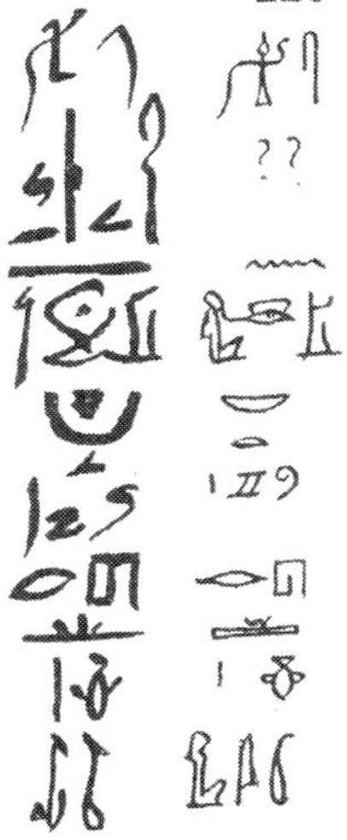

241

153

207

210
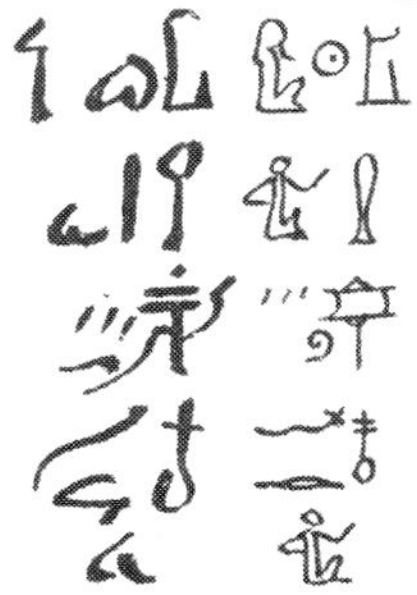

211
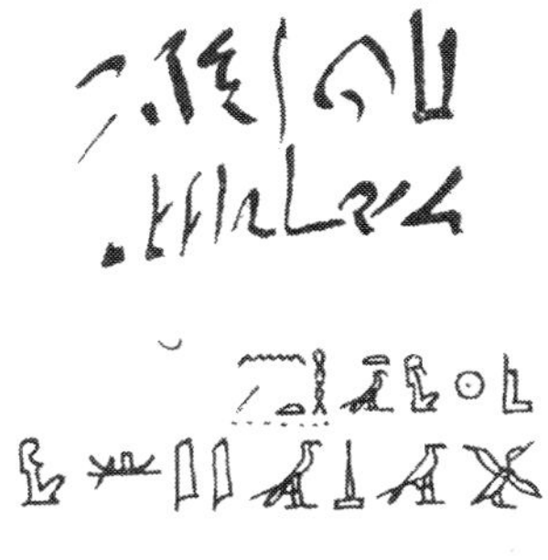

209
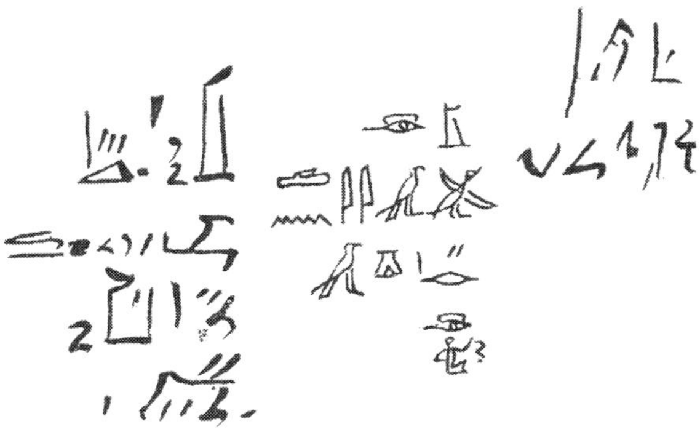

66
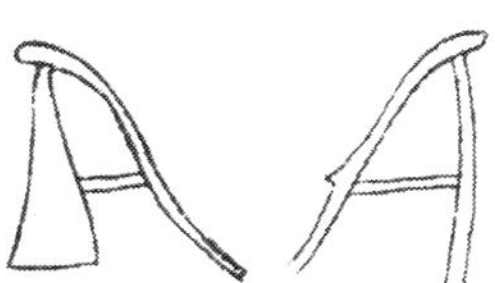

52

75
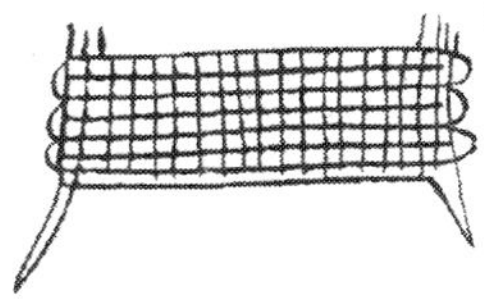

79
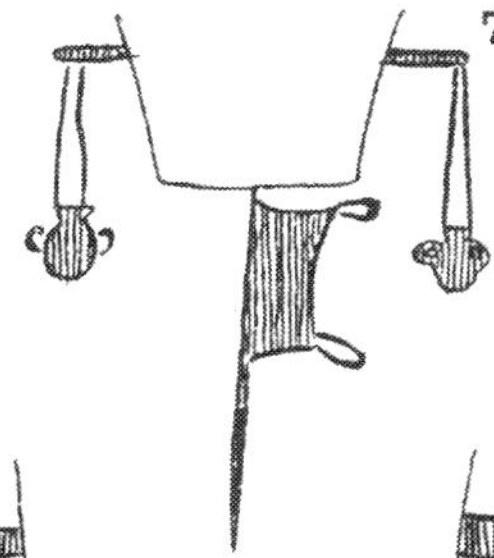

90
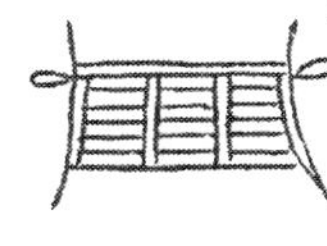

11
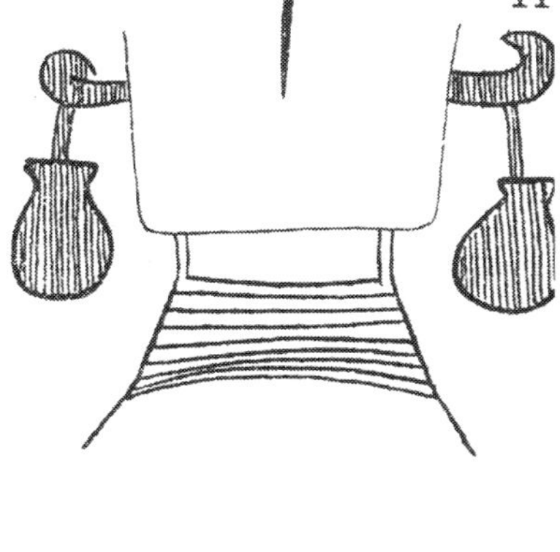

549
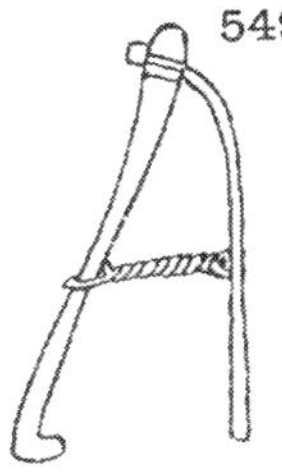

551

553
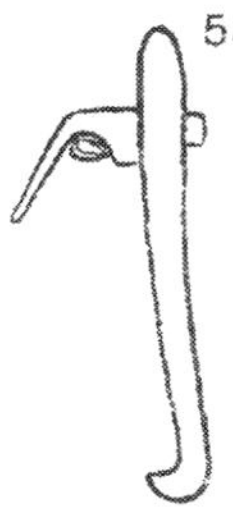

77
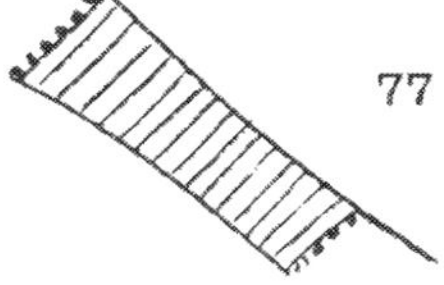

547

IN LAST COLUMN, B=BOLOGNA, B.M. BRITISH MUSEUM, C CAIRO, F FLORENCE, L LEYDEN N NAPLES, R COLLEGIO ROMANO, T TURIN, V VATICAN. MUSEUM NUMBER PRECEDES LETTER. NUMBERS WITHOUT FOLLOWING LETTER ARE IN UNIVERSITY COLLEGE.

PAINTED		INCISED
A	1 COLUMN FRONT	B
C	1 COLUMN BACK	D
E	2 COLUMNS FRONT	F
G	1 COL. FRONT, 1 BACK	H
J	COLUMNS AROUND	K
L	LINES AROUND BACK PLAIN	M
N	LINES AROUND THE WHOLE	O
P	LINES AROUND COLUMNS BACK	Q
R	LINES AROUND COLUMNS FRONT	S
T	LINES AROUND 1 COLUMN FRONT	U
V	LINES AROUND 1 COLUMN BACK	W
X	3 COLUMNS FRONT	X
Y	KILT LINES ROUND BACK	Z

a	alabaster
b	blue glaze
c	green glaze
d	other colors
e	inlayed glazes
f	schist glazed
g	granite
h	serpentine
i	sandstone
j	" painted
k	limestone plain
l	" painted
m	mud, black
n	" brown
o	" white
p	" blue or green
q	" yellow
r	pottery plain
s	" white
t	" painted
u	black steatite or marble
v	wood plain
w	" painted
x	" black
y	" inlayed
z	" incised.

2	Bandaged mummy
4	" white & red
6	No hands tools
8	Hands, no tools
	HOE PICK BASKET BAG POT
10	– – – – – – 1
12	– – – 1
14	1 – – – – – 1
16	1 – – – 1
18	1 1
20	1 1 1 TO XXIV
21	1 1 1 XXV ON
22	2 – – – – TO XXIV
23	2 – – – – XXV ON
24	2 1
26	2 BEARD
28	(BACK UNSEEN)
30	2 – – – 2
32	2 – – – – – – 2
34	2 – – 1 1
36	2 – – 1 – – 2
38	2 1 2
40	2 – – 1 1 2
42	HOLDING
	KILTED
50	arms down
52	arms folded.
54	L. down, R. whip
56	R " L "
58	with 2 hoes
60	holding
	LONG ROBE
70	L. down, R. hoe
72	L. down, R. along

α	
β	
γ	
δ	
ε	
ζ	
η	
θ	NAME ONLY
κ	TITLE AND NAME
λ	
μ	
ν	
ξ	
π	
ρ	
σ	
τ	AND CHAPTER
φ	SAME, SHORTENED
χ	SAME BLUNDERED
ψ	…
ω	HIERATIC

DATED USHABTIS. THE PRIVATE USE OF A NAME BEING 30-40 YRS AFTER ROYAL USE.

NO.		B.C.			B.C.			B.C.
46	AOHMES SAPAAR	1550	261	MYSAUHERT	1050	531	ASTNEKHEB dau Shabaka	670
47	SENEMAOH	1520	262	ASTNEKHEBT	1030	539	SHEPNEAPT	660
48	NEHI	1450	264	PANEZEM II	1006	570	HAA-AB-RA	570
65	AMENHETEP II	1423	263	HENT-TAUI	1000	546	PEF-NEFA-NET	570
80	AMENHETEP III	1379	265-6	NESIKHENSU	1000	554	AOHMES after	540
82	AKHENATEN	1365	280	UASARKEN after	900	562	AOHMES	526
86-92	SETY I	1300	464-5	" "	900	573	NET-KHADEB-AR-BENT mother NEKHT-HOR-HEB	350
93	PASER	1280	268-9	MEHTINEUSEKHT wife Uasarken II	850	599-600	NAYFOARUD	350
132	NEZEM	1250	267	MUTEMHOT wife Uasarken II	850	574-9	NEKHT-HER-HEB	342
99	KHOEMUAS	1245	283	ZED-PTAH-AUF-ONKH son Takerat II	800	635-8	HENKA born of HAKER	330
147	RAMESSU IV	1165	484	SHESHENQ III	781	641	ZEHER	320
148	" VI	1156	535-8	AMENARDAS	690	646-8	ZEHER	320
154	HENT-TAUI	1080				643-4	PEDUASAR son Zehar	300
155-7	PAINEZEM I	1074						
158-9	MAOTKARA	1070						

Lw 8τ F
ML 22τ 78T
—
var. Lv 22τ F
Ld 24φ 222
OL 24φ 65T
Ap24Ξ Ac 54Ξ F
Ar 8ρ 138
Fc 21ε B
ML 22τ V
Mk 8π 111T
GGd8πF, ML 22ν V
Ab 24Ξ 259T
Wv 8φ B
ML 8ρ 56GS1
Mv 8π B
Aw 8σ F
Ab 24λ F
715 C
Uw 74α L
Mk 8τ F
46
Pw 24τ 166
see Ab 24Ξ 356
AL8 .. 63T Av 8ν V
PL 30χ 115
Ay 8λ V
84 C
10 C
Wv 8φ F
3 C
2 C
24 C
Vd 24τ F
1 C
Mw 24τ, 132T
Eb 24Ξ 371
Ac 24λ 474
Mh 8η 535-8
Lw 22τ B
NL 22τ T
103 C
Ad 24σ B
Ad 22λ 139T
Aw24σB, Mu 30τ F
Wv 24τ F
155 C
64 C
Rw 22φ 163
R.M.A.xxxiii Kg 30τ BM
AC24K. B.244-5
Qr 6σ 58-9
Lb 24φ F
Av 8σ F
P.A.93 Ar 24ρ —
Mw 8τ 87T
179 C
SEE 295-7
Ab 24Ξ F
70 C
Ua 60τ L
Av 22σ V
Mw 22/30 τ {16T/186}
180C
Lw 24σ B
Ow 24τ 133T
Mk 8 30T
118 C
Aq 8λ V
Ab 22σ 283T
At 8Ξ F
Ov 22φ 198T
Md 6φ B

+ NEXT

Aw 22ρ 199
12 C
44 C
181 C
Qr 22σ 60
Ac 40ρ 238
Pc 24φ N
Bv 8τ B
Mw 24τ 18T
Aw 8σ B
Aw 8σ B
Aw 6σ 148-9T
Aw 6σ 89T
Lk 8π F
Aw 8σ {167/173/183} T
Aw 8σ 166T
AL 24σ 134T
Ab 24σ 282T
Ak 8Ξ 278
Mv 8π 65
23 C
Mv 8τ T
Lb 24σ 195T
Ab 24ν 244T, 277
Ab 24ν 262T
Ab {24/56} ν 248, 277-81 T
Aw 24σ B
Av 6σ 96T
LL 8τ F
Ad 36Ξ 236
Aw 8σ 182T
45,74 C
CEM.ABYD II xxxix,5 [45k]
Ad 30σ N
M bronze 6π B.M
Vw 8α 145T
ML 52ρ 51
At 24λ 144T
ML 8η F
28 C
11 C
28, 32
Bk 8λ B
Aw 24σ F
105-112 C
Ac 24Ξ 224
Br 52μ 142, Ar 24ρ 438
Ac 24,54Ξ 330-1
At,r, 24σ 434T
Nb 24φ 262
Ab 24Ξ 305
Aw 24λ 143T
Bb 24θ 531
Ua 60τ L
40 C
122 C
Aw 6μ 207
Ab 36Ξ 368
Aw 24ρ 206
At 24σ 74¾T
18 C
At. 24/38 Ξ 396
Br 24/50 Ξ 434/435
At 24Ξ 392
Ac 24Ξ 399
P.A. Br 24ρ —
Aq 24Ξ 460
Ab 24Ξ 385
Ap 24Ξ 400
Av 24Ξ —
As 24Ξ 449
168-70 C
Ap 24Ξ F406

Cc 22 Ξ 473
Ar 22 θ 461
Ac 24 Ξ 275T
Ap 24 Ξ 397
Vb 30 τ F
Aw 6 α —
Lk 8 ρ F LL 38 φ 213T
Aw 22 σ F
17 C
Ab 24 λ 272
Ab 24 Ξ 332
60 C
AL 24 Ξ 121
Ab 24 Ξ 345
Mw 8 τ 68,153T
At 24 σ 197T
Ct 58 Ξ 199T
Cc 56 σ Ξ 464-5
Ec 22 ψ 476
Ec 24 ρ 475
Kv 74 τ L
Mu 24 φ B
Ak 8 22T, At 8 λ V
At 8 ν V, At 50 σ 284/302 T
Lv 24 φ 75T
Mw 24 τ 85T
Lv 24 φ 79T
Ab 24 σ F
Bu 22 Ξ 70
Ad 42 ρ 226
AX 52 ρ 427-8
31
Aw 36 ρ 195
At 32 ν 132
Lw 36 φ 162
Aw 42 ρ 85
P.A. 105 Ab 8 —
Ab 24/54 Ξ 353/352
Vd 24 σ 230T, Px 24 σ 178T
QL 30 δ 52
Vb 24 φ 52T
Aw 32 ψ 76
161 C
Ab 58 σ B
156-7 C
2 C
57 C
Ac 54 Ξ 379
Ab 24 Ξ 356
BL 36 σ 112-3
Lv 24 τ F
Nb 24 τ 361-2
Mk 8 φ B
Ad 30 σ N
Av 22 σ 110T
Mk 8 φ 50 Mk 8 φ 50
Aw 36 ρ 191,201
Ac 24 Ξ 363
HL 24 ρ 120
Lr 6 141
Lw 22 τ B
26,29,47,92 C
214-226 C
Ac 24 Ξ F
Aw 24 λ B
Ap v 8 Ξ 407
Aw 24 ρ Ab 24 Ξ 294
At 24 λ 751T
Aw 8 σ B
Lw 24 τ B F
Ab,c, 24 Ξ —
Ap,t, 24 Ξ 393
Aw 22 λ 425

Av 24 κ F
Ac 22 ν V
Ab 24 Ξ 344 370
Ab 24 Ξ F B
Ap 22 Ξ 394
182-213 C Wv 24 τ F
Ax 24 λ 424
Mv 23/52 η N
Ab 24 λ 71 T
151 C
Ap 58 Ξ 404
Ab 14 γ 300
Aw 24 ρ 196
65 C
Eb 22/24 Ξ R.F
22 C
Ab 24 Ξ
G Ξ 351
Nb 24 φ 264
Lr 5/2 μ 153
Ab 22 σ 255
Bz 22 λ 182
102 C
Nb 24 τ F
Ar 8 λ 139
Mk 22 τ B
Lb 22 φ 282
Lb 24 φ F
Ab 24 σ 284
Ap 24 μ 458
Mk 22 ρ 56
Ac 24 Ξ 359
Jw 6 α —
ML 8 τ T
Mt 22 τ 61,62
Lb 24 ρ, 94-5 Qf 22 σ 93
Ac 24 Ξ 223
Wv 30 τ F
{ Gb 54 Ξ 53,54 C
{ Ab 24 Ξ 351/308,347
Aw 24 ρ 192
Ao 22 Ξ 447
Ap 22 Ξ 442
Ac 24/54 Ξ 376-7
Ac 24 σ 479,80
Ac 24 Ξ 372
Ab 24 ν 194T
Ac 24 κ 273
Yt 24 Ξ 382
Am 24 Ξ 451
F. Ab 24 Ξ 240T
Ac 24 μ 378
Aw 6 μ 211
Ac 24 α 469-72
Av 8 σ F
Vc 24 φ F
P.b 24 φ 274
WL 24 φ F
142 C
BL 24 λ 109
At 8 ν F
Ab 56 σ F
149-50 C
Ac 50 Ξ 151 T
At 4 Ξ 217 T
Qz 24 τ 159
Aw 24 λ B
Lc 24 τ F
Aw 6 σ T
{ Aw 24 ρ } F
Aw 8 λ N
71-2 C

160 C
Mk 8τ N
Qv 24τ 156T
178 C
87,136 C
101,114 C
4 C
Ar 8Ξ F
Ab 24Ξ F
Mc 24η F
N. Mh 22τ 532-4
Bc 24ρ 615
Ab 24 399
Ab 52Ξ 466
AS 22Ξ 445
Aw 6σ 83 T
Ac 24Ξ F
LL 24φ F
140-1 C
Bc 22Ξ B
Ah 52Ξ F
Gt 24λ 135
Aw 26σ B
Lt 24φ 742T
85 C
UL 52τ 17 T
Av 52λ F
Ma 8τ B
48 C
Ew 6δ 49
Lv 8τ F
Lw 24ρ 75
At 24σ 481,746,756T
OL 8τ 45T
31 C
Ab 24σ 261
Ac 22Ξ 558
50 C
8.9 C
Mu 30φ 66
91 C
Kk ///// F
5 C
Mw 6π B
Ab 24Ξ 270
Lw 12φ N
Av 22σ 214
19 C
76 C Qu 24ρ 71
Ab 24Ξ 288
At 50Ξ 162T
Aw 34ρ 174-5
70 C
Rw 36τ 165
Aw 24ρ 197
Aw 24ρ 217
119 C
Ac 8σ F
Ab 24Ξ 295-6
Ab 54Ξ 297
Ab 24Ξ 360
PL 36φ 106
Pw 24φ 77
Q. USARKEN II Ab 24Ξ 268-9
ML 22ρ 55
SEE Ar 22λ 128
At 22Ξ 124
Mk 22φ B
Ab 24σ 304
Ac 24Ξ 297T
At 50λ 485 515-9T

Queen USARKEN II

SEE

Aw 22Ξ, B. Ar 8ρ 436-7
Ap 24Ξ F
Mw 22τ 171T
At 24ρ 129
Ab 24κ 560-1 573 T
Ab 24Ξ 267
Aw 22ρ 200
SEE 375
94-5 C
55-9 C
115-7 C
At 24ε 130
Bz 22Ξ 103
67 C
Aw 8σ B
Wk 24τ 105T
Ap 54Ξ 403
401
Aw 24ρ 402
BL 14κ 83
Ab 24λ F
Ua 42σ B
Ui 52σ F
Uu 58ν 14T
Bk 8λ V
97 C
At 24λ F
LL 30φ 169T
LL 30τ 170T
Aw 24λ T
Mw 24τ 78T
AL 22Ξ 42T
Ab 24Ξ 336
Ac 24Ξ 365
Ac 54Ξ 335
Aw 22σ F
Ar 24λ 751T
Aw 8ρ 220
Aw 22Ξ F
Ab 22Ξ 317
Mk 8η F
SEE 45ρ BRIT. M.
AL 24σ 70T
Ou 52τ F
Aw 50σ 73T
Aw 36λ 172-3
79 C
Aw 6λ 210
Ab 24Ξ 287
Aw 22ρ 190
86 C
AL 8λ 122
ML 24τ F
Ad 8ρ 235
UL 50τ F
Hw 36σ 183-4
Wv 24τ F
Vw 8τ F
GUROB RIFEH At 24ρ 133 137
Lv 24τ 144T
Qw 24τ 167
ML 8φ B
83 C
Av 24Ξ F
Ad 24σ F
68 C
Ac 8ρ 235
153 C
{ML 22ν V
{Aw 8κ 209T
LL 24τ B
LL 8φ 66T

LL 24φ 59 57 7
Lz 8φ 157-8
QL 8σ 24 x μ 250
Aw 2λ 177
Ab 24λ F
Uu 58τ F
Mv 8π 48
Uf-b 24σ F
SEE 45C BRIT. M.
SEE 45R
Pd 24σ 227
Ao 24Ξ 457
Mf 30τ F
Wv 50τ F
Wv 50τ F
Lk 8θ T
Wa 22τ 56T
Uu 36τ L
Vw 30τ B
Bv 24γ, Fw 58σ B
Mv 8τ F
Uc 52τ B
Ap 24Ξ 405
Ab 24Ξ 322
Ao 24Ξ 456
Lb 24Ξ 275
Ab 24Ξ 298 312
Ac 24Ξ —
red face Ap 54Ξ 274T
Ac 24Ξ F—
Qz 24τ 159
Ac 24Ξ 408
Ac 24Ξ 409
Ab 24Ξ 276
Ab 24Ξ 309-10
Jc 56Ξ 234
Xb 24μ 241-2
Ab 24Ξ 292
OR Ab 24Ξ ?
Ab 24 56 Ξ 334 333
Bt 24λ 433
Ab 24Ξ 323
Ab 24Ξ 316
An 8Ξ 518
Aw 24λ 170-1, Ac 24σ 672T
Ac 8Ξ 495
Ab 24Ξ 320
Ab 24ρ 293
Ab 24Ξ 373
Ab 24Ξ 321 405
F. Ab 24Ξ 311T
Ao 24Ξ —
Ac 24Ξ 481
Ab 24Ξ —
Nb 24φ 265-6
Ap 22ν V
Ab 24Ξ 302
As 24Ξ 396
Ap 24Ξ 395
Ad 24ν N
Ab 54Ξ 350 ML 22φ 443
Ab 56Ξ —
Ap 24Ξ F
121 C
At 24λ 78
Ac 36ρ 369
Ou 52τ F
37-8, 49, 52, 125-134 C
Ac 24σ 232
Kv 50τ L
61 C
Ac 30Ξ F

69C

158 C Ac 24Ξ —
Pb 24ρ 239
46 C
Mw 24τ F
30 C
Ac 22κ 484
98 C
Ab 56γ 233
A bronze 8Ξ 3T
Ld 24τ 247
RAMESSU IV 144.5 C
Ab 24σ 258-9
Xg 52 80
4T, Aa 8σ 248
N c 24φ 88-92
Mx 24τ F, V, B. L b 24τ B
Of 24φ, F 89. Of 30ρ 87. Of 8φ 86
Ab 24ρ 260
QL 8χ —
At 8σ, AL 50Ξ 219T
Mv 6φ V
Mk 22σ 53
At 24σ 749T
Mv 22τ B
At 24λ 482T
Qz 30φ 156
Mv 8τ B
AL 58 104
Wu 8 F
Ab 24σ 367
Aq 8 V
Wv 8φ B
Bz 40ρ 181
Bg 8κ 82
Am 24μ —
143 C Ab 22σ 257
Ab 72σ 256
Mv 6π F
Av 6π 544T
Uu 8τ F
62 C. Wk 8τ F
Ar 24Ξ —
Ab 22σ B
3 C
AL 8α 40T
At 24σ 742T
Ac 24ρ 225
Au 22ν 177T
At 22ρ 123
Av 22ρ 185
Lk 8κ F
Ab 24ρ 271
Ok 6ψ F
Tv 8σ V
Aw 16ρ 220
Ac 24ν F
Ac 24Ξ 410
Et 36ψ 136
66 C
Ad 24λ B
Aw 52σ 94 T
Aw 24σ 108T
Au 8 V
Lw 32χ 168-9
Su 10σ, 100. Mk 24ρ 63
U marble 60τ L
96 C
Vb 24φ F Ab 3 5 λ 289-90
Av 42σ F
Ax 8 429. ML 22τ V
Aw 52λ 187T

Uk 60τ L
Mk 8π 111T
R.M.A. xli Qk 30τ
ML 8τ F
Aw 6σ 147T
68 C
Ad 8σ F
Ac 24σ 225
Bull shabti 104 C
AL 8σ F
50 C
63 C
Aw 22λ 176
Ax 24ρ 426
XII Dyn. SEE 45j Bk 2α C
Mw 8τ F
AL 16ρ 118-9
AL 8λ 110
Ab 24Ξ 326
Aw 24σ T 312 Ab 24Ξ 307
Nb 24φ 263
Ab 56Ξ 254
AL 22λ 54T
Ab 24Ξ —
Ab 56σ 253
Ac 24Ξ 310T. Ab 24Ξ 374
386 Ab 24Ξ 279
43 C
Ac 24Ξ 468
ML 22τ V
171-6 C
61 C
21 C
Aw 22σ F
Ab 24Ξ 301
Aw 8σ 142T
Aw 8λ 157T
Ab 24Ξ 375
E/A b 24σ {F.234T 138T
Jb 24λ F
OR ? ? Ab 24Ξ 375
Kα 24/58 φ L
box At 22ν 152
Aw 24Ξ F
At 24Ξ 340
Mc 24τ B
Ab 24Ξ 339
Ab 24λ F, Ab 24/54 Ξ 338 387
177 C
ML 30σ 107
33,34
Wv 22τ B
Mu 24σ 67
Ww 24φ F
36 C
An 8ν 454
Mw 8τ F
77 C
Bx 8Ξ F
Ab 50σ 166T
Aa 52ν 29T
At 22σ F
Uu 8e 99
Tb 30τ V
At 24σ F
154 C
At 28Ξ F
Uu 24σ B
At 24σ 747-8T
Aw 30ψ 122T

or.
OR

Ar 24ρ 12..
UL 24φ 10..
Ao 24Ξ, 4464..
At 58λ 126..
At 24Ξ 740-5..
P.A. 106 At 24Ξ —
At 24ρσ 38..
Ab 24σ L 231
27 C
Av 24σ F
45..
Vw 24τ 27T
At 58κ F
Vw 8τ 22T
4..
Bu 24Ξ 6..
Av 24ρ 21..
Aw 24ρ 19..
Ac 50λ B.L..
OL 8ρ 11..
Qz 8φ 16..
Aw 52σ F
Ad 30σ N..
159 C
A 22λ 13..
Ab 24λ F
Ab 24Ξ —
Aw 22λ 2..
Mu 22τ F
Aw 24λ ..
16 ..
Mk 8φ 4..
ML 8φ ..
6 C
42,4..
8,9 C
Cb 50σ 28..
BL 8λ 10..
Qz 30φ 7..
Lw 8φ 6T
Ab 24Ξ 34..
Mh 8η 53..
Uv 30/60 τ L
Ab 24λ F
Ar 8λ 12..
Ab 24σ 245-264
P.A. Ab 24ρ —
At 24ρ L
Wu 30τ F
Aw 6σ 158..
6 C
Mv 8τ F
Lt 36φ 7..
At 6ρ 12..
Bk 6κ 8..
Ab 22Ξ B..
99,100
Aw 56σ 140..
Ab 24Ξ 31..
13..
81..
P.A Ab 24Ξ —
Mv 8φ B..
QL 24ρ 9..
Mw 8π 112T
Av 8λ T
Mw 30φ 102..
Aw 22ρ 2..
63 C

Aw 36 ρ	198
Aw 8 Ξ	B
Aw 24 ψ	200, 203
Q r 22 φ	—
Aw 6 σ	81 T
Aw 40 ρ	178
Rw 36 τ	164
Ab 58 σ	N
As 24 Ξ	450
Bc 30 σ	N
Td 30 φ	F
{AL 22 λ 60 / Aw 24 λ 265}	T
Lv 24 φ	76 T
	88 C
Lw 24 φ	F
Ab 24/58 Ξ	357/355
Av 6 θ	30
Ab 24 Ξ	319
Aw 22 ρ	205
Ar 8 σ	F
Aw 8 ρ	219
Aw 22 Ξ	F
Ar 8 Ξ	263 T
	75 C
	41 C
Aw 8 Ξ	F
Jv 6 α	35
Ld 24 τ	F
Jv 6 α	36
Lv 24 φ	F
AL 24 σ	F
Bb 23 π	R
Awbγ, Aw6α, Ev6α	5–7
Jv6α, lid	8, 9
Gv6θ, A'v6θ, Jv6α	24–27
Jv6α, IVAv6θ, Gv6θ	18–23
Ok 22 τ	F
EB, JJLAα, JAGθ	10–17
Ac 24 Ξ	411
Mz 8 φ	73
Mk8T RMAXLi Lw 8 φ	N
Ar 22 ρ	140
Av 6 σ	84 T
Ab 56 Ξ	303
Bb 20 ρ	V
Ab 52 / Ac 24 σ	F
Ad 24 λ	F
Ab 30 ζ	F
	39 C
	32-5 C.
Uu 52 τ	21 T
Uu 58 ν	13 T
Aq 24 ν	459
Ab 24 Ξ	F, 311
Aw 60 θ	102
Ab 24 Ξ	—
	78 C
Ab 24 Ξ	306
Ab 24 Ξ	B
At 24 Ξ	384
Ab 24 Ξ	285 T
Ac 22 Ξ	366
Ab 24 Ξ	318
Ab 24 Ξ	348
At 24 Ξ	B
Ab 54 Ξ	349
Ac 24 Ξ	366
	32-5 C
Ab 24 ν	F
	80 C
	152 C

SEE

Ac 24 Ξ	485-8
Ak 22 σ	F
Ab 24 Ξ	313
Aw 8 λ	202
At 22 λ	430
	73 C
Wv 22 τ	F
	10 C
	5 C
	18 C
Av6θ 29, 29a Ac 54 Ξ	380
Mv 24 τ	F
Mk 8 τ	F
Ab 24 Ξ	324
Ac {24 ρ / 36 σ}	240 / 237
Mj 8 φ	F
At 24 σ	267 T
Ab 24 Ξ	342
Aw 24 ·	210
Ab 24 Ξ	283
Ab 24 Ξ	F
Cc 56 Ξ	427
Tu 24 τ	165 T
As 24 ρ	444
Ld 24 Ξ	F
Ac 24/56 Ξ	314/354 A
Ap 24 Ξ	F
Ab 54 Ξ	346
Ab 24 Ξ	F
Ac 22 ν	V
Ab 24 Ξ	315
Ab 24 Ξ	329
Ao 24 Ξ	243 T
Aq 8 λ	V
Am 56 Ξ	431
Ao 22 Ξ	432
Ab 24 Ξ	—
Ab 24 Ξ	493
Ab 56 Ξ	494

At 24 Ξ	440
Ar 24 σ	439
Ab 54 Ξ	280
Ah 6 λ	117
Aw 6 α	180
LL 30 χ	54
Ac 24 Ξ	
Ab 24 Ξ	291
name? Ab 24 Ξ	332
? Ab 24 Ξ	325
Ab 24 μ	243
Lb 24	381
Ap 24 Ξ	448
At 24 σ	134
Aw 24	186
At 8 ρ	125
Vc 42 φ	246
Bc 6 σ	N
Kk 8 η	R
Ld 24 φ	F
Aw 6 κ	B
Ab 54 Ξ	350

NAME PARENT

Bb 21η 617
Oc 21τ 562
Bc 23ϑ 628
Ob 21τ —
Bc 21λ 589
Sc 21ρ 602
Bc 21σ F
289-90 C
Sc 21ρ 587
Mc 21τ B
Bc 21ρ 610-11
Mc 21τ 554,559,605-6
483-506 C
Dc 21λ 621
Mh 8η 535-8
Fc 21ρ 598
Mk 21τ N
957-60 C
293-6 C
Mc 21τ B
Bc 21λ 593
Bc 21λ —
Qk 8 ζ 542
557
Bc 23λ B
246-281 C
920 C
Bc 21ρ 595
Mc 21τ F
Kk 8η R
Db 21λ 624
914-6 C
Bc 21σ N
Sc 21σ F
Sc 21σ B
Wc 21η B
905,908, C
Mc 21η B
Sc 21σ 247T
463-506 C
Bc 21σ 260-1/286 T
Bc 21ρ 584
Bc 21σ F
Bc 21σ B, F
Bc 21Ξ B
Bc 21τ F
Mc 21τ 25T
Bc 21η F
Mc 21η F
Mc 21λ B 612
Bb 21ρ 614
246-281 C
Bc 21τ F
Mc 21τ N
300-3 C
Dc 18ρ 622
599,600
963-70 C
M Bc 21φ 131T, V
482 C
Bc 21λ N
Sc 21ρ 603,608
297-9 C
963-70 C

Ob 21τ 54
Mc 21ρ F
Mc 21τ
Sc 21ρ 6
Bc 21Ξ
Oc 21η
Mc 21τ 55
fine writing Nc 21η 256-7
926
483-506
507-904
Lb 21η 64
Bb 23θ 237
Mc 21τ
Sb 21ρ 61
Sb 21σ
Mc 21τ
Mc 21τ 123
Oc 21τ 5
Bc 21
Mb 21η 93
Mc 21τ
Mc 21τ 5
Fb 21ρ 58
Mc 21τ F
Mc 21η F
558 Mc 21φ
918 C Hb 21σ
917 C
Kb 21τ
913
Mb 21τ
Db 21λ 62
Bc 21τ
Mc 21η
Mc 21τ
532-3-4 Mc 22τ, B, F
Mc 24η
Mb 21η 643
Bc 21σ
Bc 21σ
Bc 21ρ 61
Bc 21ρ 63
909-12
Bc 21η
Bc 23
Mc 21τ
Bc 21σ
Fc 21η N
963-70 C
Bb 21λ 63
Bc 21χ 61
Qc 21φ N
Bc 21σ F
Bc 21τ F
Mb 24τ N
377-506 C
292 C
Fc 21ρ 59
Mc 21τ 28/125 T
Ab 22 64

907 C
Sc21σ F
Mc21T 5 NT
Bc23Ξ B
291 C
574 Mc21T 575-6-9
Oc21T 543
Kb21T 545
906 C
Bc21σ B
Mb21π 573
Bc21λ B
Mc21T 570
Bc21ρ 591
Bc23ρ V
Sc21ρ F
Bc21η B
Ac21λ 137T
Mb21T 48T
Sc21ρ 607
Mc21T V
Mc21T B
Mc21T 150T B F
Mc21T B
Sb21σ 580
Bc21σ B
Mc21 19T
Uc21σ B
Bc21σ B
Mb21T 571
Bc21σ B
Mc21T B
Bc21λ B
Mc21T B
Oc21χ —
Mc21T N
Mc21π 24T
Mh21η 540
D basalt 72Ξ 117T
Dc23Ξ 825
Sb21σ N
Mc21T B
Fc23Ξ V
Mc21T B
12IT Mb21T B 567,586
XXX DYN.
Hb23ρ 635-8
919 C
282-8 C
Bc21Ξ B
Sc21ρ 583
304-376 C
Bc21λ B
Dc21λ 623
Bc21 585
Mc21T 563
Ub21σ B
Mc21T N
Mc21T 560

Bc21σ B
547-53
Sc21σ BN
Mc21T 200T
Mc21T 104T
Bc21σ B
Bc21σ B
928 C
Ac21ρ 620
Bc21σ B
Ab21φ 161T
Kb21Ξ 12,21T B
Mb24T N
Qc21T —
Mb21T 561
Ob21η —
Mb21T 569
Mb21T 572
Mc21T F
Mc21η
483-506 C
Dc21μ
Bc21σ F
963-970 C
Mc21T 214T
539
Kc21T F.B
Sc21σ B
Bb21λ 592
Dc23σ 258T
Bb21λ B
Hc21σ B
Bc21T F
Bc21σ N
Oc21φ 568
Mb21φ 577
Bb21K B
Av6σ 84T
Mc21φ B
Bc21ρ 594-6-7
Ab70α 242T
Hc23λ T
Fc21ρ 601
Bc21ρ 544
Bc21T F
Lb21η 196T
Mb21T 564
Ab24 646-8
Bc24ρ 641
Mc21T 565-6
Sc21Ξ F
Bc21σ N
Bc21σ 590
Bc21λ 588

1
2
3
4
3A
9
5
6
7
8
10
11
13
12
14

15
16
17
18
19
20
21
22
23
24
25
26
27
28
29
29 A

30
31
32
33
34
35
36
37
38
39
40
41
42
43
44
45

47
48
49
53
51
52
50
54
55
56

58
59
60
61
62
63
64
64 A
65
66
67
68
69
70
71
72

73
74
75
76
77
78
79
80
81
82
97
83

87
88
89
93
85
86
90
91
92
94
95
96
97
98
99
100
101
102
103
104
105
106
107
108
109

110
111
112
113
114
115
116
117
118
119
120
121
122

123
124
125
126
127
128
129
130
131
132
133
134
135
136
137
138
139
140
141
142

145
146
147
148
149
150
151
156
157
159
158
160
161
162
163
164
165
166
167
168
169

152
153

231
232
233
234
235
222
223
224
225
226
237
238
239
240
241
242
243

246
247
248
249
250
251
252
253
255
254
256
257
259
258
260
261
262
263
264
265
266

1 : 2

USHEBTIS GLAZED, XXIST DYN.

335
336
337
338
339
340
341
344
345
346
347
348
342
343
349
352
353
354
355
356
357
358
359
360
361
362

363
354A
365
366
367
368
369
370
375
385
386
387
388
390
391
392
395
401
402
406
407
408
412
413
414
415

424
425
426
427
430
431
432
433
434
435
436
437
438
439
440
442
443
444
445
446
447
448

1:2

USHEBTIS GLAZED OR PAINTED, XXIST TO XXIIIRD DYN.

531
532
533
534
535
536
539
540
543
542
544
545
546
547
549
550

554
555
556
557
558
559
560
561
562
563
564
565
567
568
569
570
571
572
57

574
576
577
578
580
582
583
584
585
586
587
588
589
590
593
594
595
596
598
599
602
603

604
605
610
612
613
614
615
616
617
618
642
645
644
643
646
647
649
650
651
652
656